Research Reports ESPRIT

Project 688 · AMICE · Vol. 1

Edited in cooperation with
the Commission of the European Communities

ESPRIT Consortium AMICE (Eds.)

Open System Architecture for CIM

Springer-Verlag
Berlin Heidelberg New York
London Paris Tokyo Hong Kong

Editors

ESPRIT Consortium AMICE
489 Avenue Louise, Bte. 14
B-1050 Brussels, Belgium

ESPRIT-Project 688, AMICE, A European Computer Integrated Manufacturing Architecture, belongs to Subprogramme 5, Computer Integrated Manufacturing (CIM), of ESPRIT, the European Stratetic Programme for Research and Development in Information Technology supported by the European Communities.

The aim of this project was to design an open system architecture for CIM (CIM-OSA) and to define a set of concepts and rules to facilitate the building of future CIM systems. Migration paths are provided for the evolution of already installed CIM subsystems. An important aspect of the project is its direct involvement in standardization activities and liaisons with other ESPRIT or similar projects, especially those that are directly related to architectural issues.

Under the management of ESPRIT Consortium AMICE, 21 companies from 7 European countries are cooperating in the project.

ISBN 978-3-540-52058-0
DOI 10.1007/978-3-642-97220-1

ISBN 978-3-642-97220-1 (eBook)

Softcover reprint of the hardcover 1st edition 1989

Printing and Binding: Weihert-Druck GmbH, Darmstadt
2145/3140 – 543210 – Printed on acid-free paper

ABSTRACT

The objective of computer integrated manufacturing (CIM) is the appropriate integration of the information exchange within a company with the help of computer aided tools. Integration includes the physical and logical connection of processes by means of data communications technology operating to specified standards, but also the integration of enterprise functions and enterprise information.

To reduce the complexity to a manageable level a structuring concept has to be provided to allow a common understanding of the subject. Generalized models are required to identify the principal components, processes, constraints and information sources used to describe a manufacturing business progressing towards CIM. The generalised models then need to be made specific by including aspects from particular manufacturing segmentations. Such a structured concept or architecture is called an Open System Architecture.

An Open System Architecture should provide:

* a general definition of the scope and nature of CIM,
* guidelines for implementation,
* a description of constituent systems and subsystems,
* a modular framework complying with international standards.

As the need for an Open System Architecture was recognized, Project 688 CIM-OSA was launched within the ESPRIT programme and the ESPRIT Consortium AMICE established. Twenty-one companies from seven European countries are cooperating in the project, which started in 1986. Nearly every major IT vendor in Europe is represented in the consortium along with major CIM users such as automotive and aerospace companies. Also CIM implementors such as software houses are members of the consortium, and the university research and development area is represented.

The objective of the project is to develop an Open System Architecture. This includes defining requirements and building blocks, and specifying a method for migrating to CIM-OSA. Also standardization activities are part of the objective of the consortium.

ESPRIT Consortium AMICE
489 Avenue Louise, Bte. 14
B - 1050 Brussels, Belgium

Phone....: +32-2-647 31 75
Fax......: +32-2-648 99 49
Telex....: +046-63 370

AEG AEG AKTIENGESELLSCHAFT
Hahnstrasse 30-32
D - 6000 FRANKFURT 71

aerospatiale AEROSPATIALE
37 Bd Montmorency
F - 75781 PARIS Cedex 16

ALCATEL ALCATEL NV
Excelsiorlaan 71
B - 1930 ZAVENTEM

APT NEDERLAND BV APT NEDERLAND BV
Larenseweg 50 - P.O. 1168
NL - 1200 HILVERSUM

BRITISH AEROSPACE BRITISH AEROSPACE plc
Brooklands Road - Weybridge
SURREY KT13OSj - ENGLAND

Bull BULL S A
121. Avenue Malakoff
F - 75116 PARIS

CAP GEMINI SESA CAP GEMINI SESA Belgium *
Bld de la Woluwe 2
B - 1150 BRUXELLES

  DIGITAL EQUIPMENT GmbH
Freischuetzstrasse 91
D - 8000 MUENCHEN 81

 Dornier DORNIER Luftfahrt GmbH
Postfach 1420
D - 7990 FRIEDRICHSHAFEN 1

 FIAT FIAT S p A
Corso G Marconi 10/20
I - 10125 TORINO

GEC GEC Electrical Projects Ltd
Boughton Road - Rugby
WARWICKSHIRE CV 21 1BU - ENGLAND

hp HEWLETT PACKARD FRANCE
HEWLETT PACKARD
Boulevard Steve Biko
F - 38090 VILLEFONTAINE

IBM IBM DEUTSCHLAND GmbH
Pascalstrasse 100
D - 7000 STUTTGART 80

iCL INTERNATIONAL COMPUTERS Ltd / ICL House
1, High Street
PUTNEY London SW15 1SW - ENGLAND

ITALSIEL ITALSIEL
Via Isonzo 21/B
I - 00100 ROMA

PHILIPS N.V MBLE S.A Philips
Rue des deux Gares 82
B - 1070 BRUSSELS

P PROCOS A/S
PROCOS AS
Bregnerodvej 144
DK - 3460 BIRKEROD

 SEIAF S.E.I A F SPA
Via Garaventa 2
I - 16121 GENOVA

SIEMENS SIEMENS AKTIENGESELLSCHAFT
Otto-Hahn-Ring 6
D - 8000 MUENCHEN 83

VW VOLKSWAGEN AG
D - 3180 WOLFSBURG

WZL TH AACHEN WZL-AACHEN UNIVERSITY
Lab. of Machine Tools / Steinbachstrasse 53B
D - 5100 AACHEN

* PRIME CONTRACTOR

TABLE OF CONTENTS

Introduction...1

1. Management Overview..8
   1.1 Reasons for CIM-OSA...8
      1.1.1 The Problems in Manufacturing Industry.....................8
      1.1.2 The Problems in Information Technology......................9
      1.1.3 Future Needs in Manufacturing Industry....................10
      1.1.4 The Integration Problems and Their Solutions.11
   1.2 CIM-OSA Overview...13
      1.2.1 Scope and Goal of CIM-OSA................................13
      1.2.2 CIM-OSA Objectives and Requirements.......................14
   1.3 Content of CIM-OSA...16
      1.3.1 The CIM-OSA Framework.....................................17
      1.3.2 Main Components of CIM-OSA................................21
   1.4 Applying CIM-OSA...27
   1.5 CIM-OSA Relation to State of the Art...........................28
   1.6 Project Results and Status of CIM-OSA..........................29
      1.6.1 Current Level of Validation and
            Applicability..29
      1.6.2 Current Level of Involvement in
            Standardization..29
      1.6.3 Future Contributions to CIM-OSA..........................30
   1.7 Benefits of CIM-OSA..30

2. Project Perspective..31
   2.1 Before AMICE...31
   2.2 Starting AMICE...32
   2.3 The AMICE Project..33
   2.4 After AMICE..34
   2.5 List of Participating Members..................................35

3. Introduction to CIM-OSA...39
   3.1 Architectural Principles.......................................39
   3.2 Structuring Concepts...40
   3.3 Relation of CIM-OSA to the Real World..........................40

4. CIM-OSA Architectural Model.......................................42
   4.1 Architectural Framework of CIM-OSA.............................44
      4.1.1 Levels of Genericity and Stepwise
            Instantiation..46
      4.1.2 Levels of Modelling and Stepwise Derivation..49
      4.1.3 Levels of Views and Stepwise Generation....52
   4.2 CIM-OSA Models...53
   4.3 CIM-OSA Relation to State of the Art...........................54
   4.4 Architecture Summary...56

5. The CIM-OSA Modelling Levels......................................58
   5.1 CIM-OSA Requirements Definition Modelling Level....60
      5.1.1 Function View..60
      5.1.2 Information View...68
      5.1.3 Resource View..71
      5.1.4 Organisation View..71

5.2 CIM-OSA Design Specification Modelling Level.......71
   5.2.1 Function View................................72
   5.2.2 Information View.............................72
   5.2.3 Resource View...............................75
   5.2.4 Organisation View...........................75
5.3 CIM-OSA Implementation Description Modelling Level.78
   5.3.1 System Description Manufacturing Technology
      Components....................................80
   5.3.2 System Description Information Technology
      Components....................................80
   5.3.3 Function View...............................80
   5.3.4 Information View.............................81
   5.3.5 Resource View...............................87
   5.3.6 Organisation View...........................89
   5.3.7 CIM-OSA Environments.........................92

6. **The Parts of the CIM-OSA Framework and Their Relations.**95
  6.1 CIM-OSA Architectural Levels......................95
  6.2 CIM-OSA Modelling and View Levels.................95
  6.3 CIM-OSA View Level Constructs and Their Relations..96
   6.3.1 Function View...............................96
   6.3.2 Information View.............................99
   6.3.3 Resource View..............................101
   6.3.4 Organisation View..........................101

7. **Detailed Description of CIM-OSA.**....................103
  7.1 CIM-OSA Requirements Definition Modelling Level
   Constructs..103
   7.1.1 Business Process Event......................103
   7.1.2 Business Process...........................103
   7.1.3 Business Process Result.....................104
   7.1.4 Procedural Rule Set........................104
   7.1.5 Declarative Rule...........................105
   7.1.6 Enterprise Activity........................106
  7.2 CIM-OSA Information Model.........................107
   7.2.1 Information View - Instantiation Process....109
   7.2.2 Information View - Derivation Process.......109
   7.2.3 Components of the Information View..........110
  7.3 CIM-OSA Implementation Description Modelling Level
   Constructs..112
   7.3.1 Functional Entity Content..................112
   7.3.2 Functional Entity Communication............114
   7.3.3 Functional Entities, Transactions, and
      Protocols....................................116
  7.4 CIM-OSA Integrating Infrastructure (IIS)..........117
   7.4.1 Concepts of the Architecture of the IDPE....117
   7.4.2 Overview of the Resulting IDPE Architecture.122
   7.4.3 Communications Management (CM) Service......129
   7.4.4 The System Wide Exchange (SE) Service.......133
   7.4.5 The System Wide Data (SD) Service...........137
   7.4.6 The Data Management (DM) Service............140
   7.4.7 The Machine Front End Service...............142
   7.4.8 The Human Front End (HF) Service............150
   7.4.9 The Application Front End Service...........163

    7.4.10 The Business Process Control (BC) Service..170
    7.4.11 The Activity Control (AC) Service..........176
    7.4.12 The Resource Management (RM) Service.......181
    7.4.13 IIS Relation to State of the Art..........188
    7.4.14 Reference Architecture and Standardisation.188

8. CIM-OSA System Life Cycle............................190
  8.1 Product Life Cycles..............................190
  8.2 System Life Cycle................................191
  8.3 Relationships Between the Product and System Life
     Cycles...192
  8.4 Contents of System Life Cycles..................193
    8.4.1 Phase A - System Requirements Specification.195
    8.4.2 Phase B - System Design.....................197
    8.4.3 Phase C - System Build and Release..........199
    8.4.4 Phase D - System Operation..................200
  8.5 Relation of System Life Cycle to the CIM-OSA
     Framework..200

9. CIM-OSA Business Process Design and Execution.........202
  9.1 Business Process Design and Maintenance...........202
  9.2 CIM-OSA Run Time - Business Process Execution.....204
  9.3 Example of Business Process Design................205
    9.3.1 Step 1: Select Business Process Type........205
    9.3.2 Step 2: Identify Business Process Content...206
    9.3.3 Step 3: Design Procedural Rule Set..........206
  9.4 Example of Business Process Execution.............207
    9.4.1 Step 1: Start Business Process Execution....208
    9.4.2 Step 2: Select Enterprise Activity Inputs...208

10. Results from Standardisation Efforts..................210

List of Figures..212

INTRODUCTION

On Integration

Computer applications have by now entered almost all enterprises, but mostly in an uncoordinated way without long term integration plans or automation strategies. Departments introduced computing equipment and purchased or developed programs to support their department operations. This approach divided an enterprise into small and almost autonomous enterprises, each with the goal to deploy the computer to make their department and its associated activities work more efficiently.

Thus many departments acquired computers, developed and installed automation systems and PCs and educated their staff, announcing this was done to make the work force aware of the large benefits that computers bring. In this fashion the most important functions in an enterprise were more or less computerized (accounting more, CAM and CAD less). In 1986 Europe, the level of computerization in descending order of significance was as follows:

Accounting, Inventory Control, Order Entry, Production Planning & Control, Purchasing, Distribution, Sales Planning, Shop Floor Control, Process Control, Quality Control, Manufacturing Engineering (including CAM), and finally Design Engineering (with CAD) [1].

The net result (something that dawned upon us after decades) was that the enterprise consisted of many "islands of automation". Moreover, these islands could even be found within departments, where specific functions had been computerized without regard to the impact on the remainder. In the late seventies it became clear that smooth transfer of information between enterprise activities and even within departments was a burden, if at all possible.

Since information management exists only in the minds of a few, we rarely know what information is stored where, and for whom it was intended. Strategic and technical information is still recreated many times, and differences between versions sometimes lead to industrial catastrophes. Millions have been invested in materials and machinery that weren't used or needed because of wrong or misinterpreted information.

Consequently, the first moves towards integration were made to study integration possibilities between the functions. The initial efforts yielded only partial success since partial solutions were looked for, like 'integration' between Sales planning and Production planning, Process control and Quality control, to name just some attempts to build bridges between islands of automation.

The design engineering area had the greatest need for **integration** of automation islands. Here technical data are converted into product structures and in turn yield parts lists. These are used by the purchasing department, the logisticians, the material handling offices, the manufacturing and design engineering groups, etc.

Therefore, remarkably, integration activities were first stimulated between Design engineering and Manufacturing engineering, the two enterprise functions that were the least computerized.

Although the approach taken seems chaotic and far from logical, we must realize that integration is nowadays centered around the computerized Master Production Scheduling systems installed in most manufacturing companies. These scheduling systems contain the complete set of bills-of-material, and in creating integration, we have at least a catalyst. It would have been more logical, however, to center integration activities around the design engineering information and the information on purchased materials. The latter two functions are responsible for more than 60% of the information in a manufacturing firm.

All these elaborate and time-consuming integration efforts will remain without the expected results if we continue to neglect some very important aspects in modern manufacturing. The comparatively low levels of automation introduced in the past were often managed entirely by members of a single discipline. The current levels of automation need broader levels of knowledge and therefore require the involvement of a wide range of professional disciplines leading to multi-disciplinary teams. Such teams have to include not only production engineers and computer specialists, but also product designers, production control experts, telecommunication experts, logisticians, material managers, human factors specialists, etc.

The resulting technical and organizational problems are compounded by the multiplicity of equipment required on the manufacturing floor and even in the office. Many problems arise because no single vendor (not even a single industry) can supply all of the many different products and services required for a modestly high-level automation project.

On Architecture

While everybody in CIM recognizes that CIM comprises many separate modules and sub-systems that have to fit into an overall framework, there is no generally agreed solution for the required architectural structure.

We refer to an architecture as a structured composition that can be viewed as the basis for the definitions of a product or an organization. Additionally, this composition contains the rules and the definitions of the properties of all constituent **parts**. With the rules and the defined properties, the parts are linked, and result in a **whole**. Thus our defined term **integration** is an implicit aspect of an architecture: through rules, the defined properties of seemingly unrelated parts are integrated into a whole.

The parts considered are: the people we employ, the machines used to manufacture our products, the computers we install for different applications, the storage wherein all relevant information is contained, and the data communication means required to insure that all the parts can be physically interconnected. In addition, we need procedures, rules and methods to make certain that all information generated or needed by the constituent parts can be interchanged. The planning control, cost calculations and various maintenance functions should support the parts; and thus must have access to all physical and information processing activities of the parts and the whole. With an appropriate set of rules and definitions of the properties of all these parts, we can now structure the plan. The plan contains all interrelationships between the parts, and the information that has to be interchanged (via well defined interfaces) to enable all parts to work as one whole, or one enterprise.

In the various aspects of the CIM-OSA specification that we will discuss in this book, these are the essential parts that will be treated:

- the CIM-OSA architectural concepts and framework
- its modelling levels
- constituent parts of the framework and their relations
- detailed descriptions of parts of the architecture
- the CIM-OSA life-cycle
- the Business Process design and execution, and
- the results from the standardization work.

The Project Formal Reference Base, a very detailed technical definition of CIM-OSA concepts and constructs, is the base for this book. Those interested in this Reference Base can fill in the order form included in this book to receive the information.

On the Project

The need for a CIM architecture was recognized in the ESPRIT programme of the European Commission (CEC) and led to the formation of a European consortium of manufacturing enterprises for the development of such an architecture. The AMICE consortium was founded in 1984 as a conglomerate of four consortia which had submitted proposals for architecture development under the ESPRIT Programme. The Consortium currently consists of:

AEG (D), AEROSPATIALE (F), ALCATEL (B), APT NEDERLAND (NL), BRITISH AEROSPACE (GB), BULL (F), CAP SESA (B), DEC (D), DORNIER (D), FIAT (I), GEC (GB), HP (F), IBM (D), ICL (GB), ITALSIEL (I), MBLE-PHILIPS (B), PROCOS (DK), S.E.I.A.F (I), SIEMENS (D), VOLKSWAGEN (D), WZL-AACHEN UNIVERSITY (D).

The overall project is supervised by the AMICE Management Committee (AMC) consisting of representatives of the constituent parties. The AMC handles contractual, strategic and financial matters and is responsible for the allocation of resources. The daily management is carried out by a full-time project director who is assisted by a small staff for administrative, planning and clerical activities. An executive committee (five persons) reviews periodically the project's progress with the project director. This executive board makes decisions about items that need immediate attention and action, and reports to the AMC.

Central staff and some of the technical work activities are concentrated at one location in Brussels. This has proven essential for the entire operation.

Technical work is carried out in 10 Work Packages employing currently a total of 60 people from all participating organisations.

An important aspect of the project is its direct involvement in standardization activities and liaisons with other ESPRIT or similar projects, especially those that are directly related to architectural issues. Close liaisons exist with the European MAP Users Group, the European Workshop for Open Systems, the CEN/CENELEC Expert Group on Information Technology for Advanced Manufacturing, and ISO/TC184.

The output of the project consists of these types:

* Project deliverables containing detailed descriptions of the results of the project. The deliverables refer to a wealth of foreground and background documents that have either been generated or used during the project.

* Public documents describing the project results in less technical jargon, and for wide distribution.

* Presentations and publications on topics related to the methodologies developed in the project. These are presented and published in the course of exhibitions, conferences, workshops, etc.

* A comprehensive interactive demonstration model of the architecture implemented on a small range of selected workstations. The demonstration model is continuously updated to include the latest developments of the CIM-OSA architecture.

* An animated demonstration running on personal computers (PC-AT), explaining all the essential features of the architecture. Interested readers may obtain a version of the CIM-OSA AD/0.5 story board by filling out the earlier mentioned order form.

The project work under ESPRIT I will end with year-end 1989. It is expected that work will continue under an ESPRIT II contract, resulting in a set of definitive specifications for CIM-OSA products.

On the Book

With the publication of this book we aim to:

* **promote the CIM-OSA and its underlying concepts**

* **enlarge the circle of interested organizations**

* **educate the Manufacturing and Information Technology community at large**

This book reports on results obtained in ESPRIT project no. 688. It describes the concepts and constructs of CIM-OSA AD/0.5 (Architecture Description). Publication of the detailed descriptions of CIM-OSA is considered very important by the ESPRIT Consortium AMICE. We must address all of our industry and the educational system to familiarise them with the concepts and the associated solutions of a true architecture for Computer Integrated Manufacturing. Only through the most widespread knowledge and awareness can acceptance of such a new concept as CIM-OSA be reached.

Therefore this book addresses: information managers, information planners, CAD, CAM and CIM oriented engineers, logisticians, software engineers, systems architects and system analysts. Large parts of the book should also be read by development and manufacturing engineers, efficiency and organization consultants, material managers, automation professionals in the financial and administrative sectors, and product and production planners. Finally, managers on all levels of the organizations of manufacturing enterprises are invited to read the book.

Of course, everyone involved in the educational process focusing on Information Technology must become familiar with the contents of CIM-OSA AD/0.5 as well.

The work of the AMICE consortium can be considered 'in-process' because much detailing, verifying, integrating and using the discussed specification are still required. Nevertheless, operations are well under way and are proceeding with dedication, leading to new versions of CIM-OSA which will be published in due course.

The final goal of Computer Integrated Manufacturing is to create a powerful integration technology. This technology will have as its foundation a spacious, competent architecture based on solid rigorous characteristics and methods, and contain all the available standardization efforts for which CIM-OSA provides a stable base.

The definition development and validation of a CIM architecture involves an enormous effort. This effort requires close collaboration and support from the companies in the AMICE consortium, the future users and the concerned Information Technology supply industries.

We gratefully acknowledge the support and enthusiastic motivation received from the officials of the European Community, without whom we could not have obtained the results presented in this book. Equally important is the acknowledgement of all the excellent contributions made by the project participants. Without their dedication to the work and their willingness to cooperate in spite of organizational, cultural and national differences the current state of this work would not have been achieved.

Brussels, August 1989

on behalf of the ESPRIT Consortium AMICE

Kurt Kosanke   Jakob Vlietstra
Project Director   Chairman - AMICE Management Committee

References

[1] De Meyer: The Integration of Information Systems in Manufacturing
Omega, Int. Journal of Management Sciences 15(3):229-238, 1987

AMICE Publications

[1] AMICE Project Team: CIM-OSA: Reference Architecture Specification
Esprit Consortium AMICE, Brussels, Belgium, 1988

[2] AMICE Project Team: CIM-OSA: A Primer on Key Concepts and Purpose
Esprit Consortium AMICE, Brussels, Belgium, 1987

[3] AMICE Project Team: CIM-OSA: Strategic Management and Design Issues
Esprit Consortium AMICE, Brussels, Belgium, 1987

[4] J. Huysentruyt, P. Russell: CIM-OSA: Computer Integrated Manufacture-Open System Architecture
Esprit Technical Week 86, Brussels, Belgium

[5] P. Russell: Open System Architecture for CIM
CIM Europe Conference 87, Knutsford, UK

[6] J.C. Emond, T. Hermans: CIM-OSA Concepts Demonstrated with an Object Oriented Language
CIM Europe Conference 88, Madrid, Spain

[7] S. Moss: CIM-OSA: The Enterprise Model
CIM Europe Conference 88, Madrid, Spain

[8] M. Klittich: CIM-OSA: The Implementation Viewpoint
CIM Europe Conference 88, Madrid, Spain

[9] J.C. Emond: CIM-OSA: Key Concepts Overview and Demonstration
Esprit Technical Week 88, Brussels, Belgium

[10] M. Klittich: CIM-OSA and its Relationship to MAP
CIM Europe Conference 89, Athens, Greece

[11] T. Klevers: The European Approach to an "Open Systems Architecture" for CIM
CIM Europe Conference 89, Athens, Greece

[12] Dirk Beeckman: CIM-OSA: Computer Integrated Manufacturing-Open Systems Architecture
Int. Journal of Computer Integrated Manufacturing 2(2):94-106, 1989

1. Management Overview

1.1 Reasons for CIM-OSA

The manufacturing process, i.e. the transformation of raw material into marketable products is changing from a semi-stable process to a highly dynamic one. The reasons for this change are manifold and only some of the major reasons are listed in the following:

o   World-wide availability of technology, capital and information (know-how) leads to short development cycles for new products.

o   World-wide marketing of products leads to strong cost competition in established markets.

o   Fast changes in market demands leads to fast obsolescence of established products

The result for the manufacturing industry at large is an upcoming era of permanent change in its economic and technology environment.

To cope with this permanent change is the major future challenge for the manufacturing industry. For each company the challenge is to stay synchronized with the external changes; i.e. to have an adaptation cycle shorter than the external one.

Manufacturing companies have started to face the new challenges by introducing new concepts like Just in Time, Continuous Flow, Kanban, to name a few. However CIM is viewed to bring the real solution to the manufacturing industry.

1.1.1 The Problems in Manufacturing Industry

Today the manufacturing industry still strives for stability of its production system as a major enterprise goal. Therefore, Management of Change is not yet considered a permanent objective in the manufacturing industry.

Information processing is still very much fragmented even in computerized applications. This is due to past bottom up generation of computer applications, to the use of multi-vendor hardware and software and to the organizational boundaries in the companies as well.

Therefore, the decision making process in the companies is still based on traditional information processing -

information gathering with 'paper and pencil', on request and from inconsistent sources. This process is at the least very time consuming. In many cases it yields only insufficient or even outright wrong information.

Simulation of alternative solutions is not possible today on a larger scale. Neither can solutions be easily and adequately described for computer processing nor is the quality of available information sufficient for simulation.

In addition, the companies are not organized for fast decision making processes. Departments are still managed according to their own sub-goals rather than to real enterprise goals. The responsibilities are still structured in one-dimensional hierarchies which mix responsibilities for enterprise assets with those for enterprise operations. Matrix organization is still a theoretical concept.

To summarise, the problems of the manufacturing industry are:

o   Lack of awareness for the new challenges

o   Insufficient enterprise organization

o   Inaccessibility of available information

o   Inconsistency of available information

o   Insufficient Processability (simulation) of available information

1.1.2 The Problems in Information Technology

It is the expectation of the industry that CIM will improve enterprise competitiveness through:

o   Adaptability and flexibility of enterprise operation and organisation

o   Efficient use of enterprise assets/resources: People, Capital Investments and Information

To reach this goal information technology provides a very important and powerful tool for the enterprise. However, a tool which still needs further improvements before it will fulfil the high expectations. CIM-OSA will bring many of the improvements required for reaching the high goals of CIM.

Information Technology hardware makes it possible even today to install very large networks of computer systems with almost unrestricted performance and processing capabilities.

What is missing is the necessary software which allows a meaningful processing of the vast amount of information needed and existing in the manufacturing enterprise. This meaningful processing, i.e. the processing of the right information, for the right purpose, at the right time, in the right place is still the major problem in information technology application.

Todays computer applications have been developed as standalone units. Functional aspects, information and data aspects and even organisational aspects are part of the application. In addition portability is limited since most of the applications are implemented on proprietary hardware and software.

The development and especially the maintenance of computer applications still present major problems, in terms of overall effort involved, and elapsed time. The reason for this is that applications are essentially produced in a **hand crafted** fashion without any real common standards, methods or tools. A real **Industrial Approach** is needed to replace the craft of application development.

Application software and its development are not the only weak points in the application of information technology. Another one is the problem of information integration, i.e. the ability to access information generated and used by different applications, running on different computer systems.

To summarise, the problems of information technology are:

o   Computer application development and maintenance is a major bottle-neck in the use of information systems.

o   Information exchange between existing computer applications is hampered by the incompatibility of applications.

o   Portability of computer applications across different vendor systems is reduced by the incompatibility of those systems.

1.1.3 Future Needs in Manufacturing Industry

To cope with the permanent change of the environment the enterprise has to be able to manage in 'real time' the required internal changes. i.e. to keep the internal adaptation shorter than the external change cycle.

This requires the 'real time' control of the whole manufacturing process from material source to product service in the market. It requires the ability to make decisions in 'real time' as well.

To establish the required fast decision making process all responsibilities in a company have to be visible. This will not be the equivalent of todays organization chart but will be the explicit knowledge about all decision making individuals in the company and about their explicit responsibilities.

To support the decision making process the right information has to be accessible in time and the results of the decision making process have to be available in the right place. Decision making also has to take into account alternative solutions and their possible impacts on the total enterprise operation. Therefore, processable description and simulation of those alternative solutions is another requirement on future decision support systems.

To summarise, the future needs of the manufacturing industry are:

o   Ability to manage in view of permanent change of the environment

o   Real time control of total manufacturing process (from supplier material input to product service at customer)

o   Adaptability and flexibility of the total enterprise (operation and organization)

o   Explicitly processable, functional and dynamic-behavioural description of the total enterprise (for simulation and real time operation control).

o   Availability of the right information in the right place at the right time

o   Ability to employ Information Technology according to its inherent capabilities rather than to the modelling of past and present information processing methods.

o   Ability to source equipment from different vendors

These needs are paramount for the survival of many manufacturing companies. To satisfy these needs is the reason for CIM-OSA.

1.1.4 The Integration Problems and Their Solutions

Integration is expected to solve many of the problems in the manufacturing industry. However, integration is understood in many different ways by the people in the industry (Figure 1-1).

o   The users expects CIM to provide integration of information in terms of availability, accessibility and consistency.
o   The vendors see system integration in terms of system connectivity and portability of computer application as the main goal of CIM.

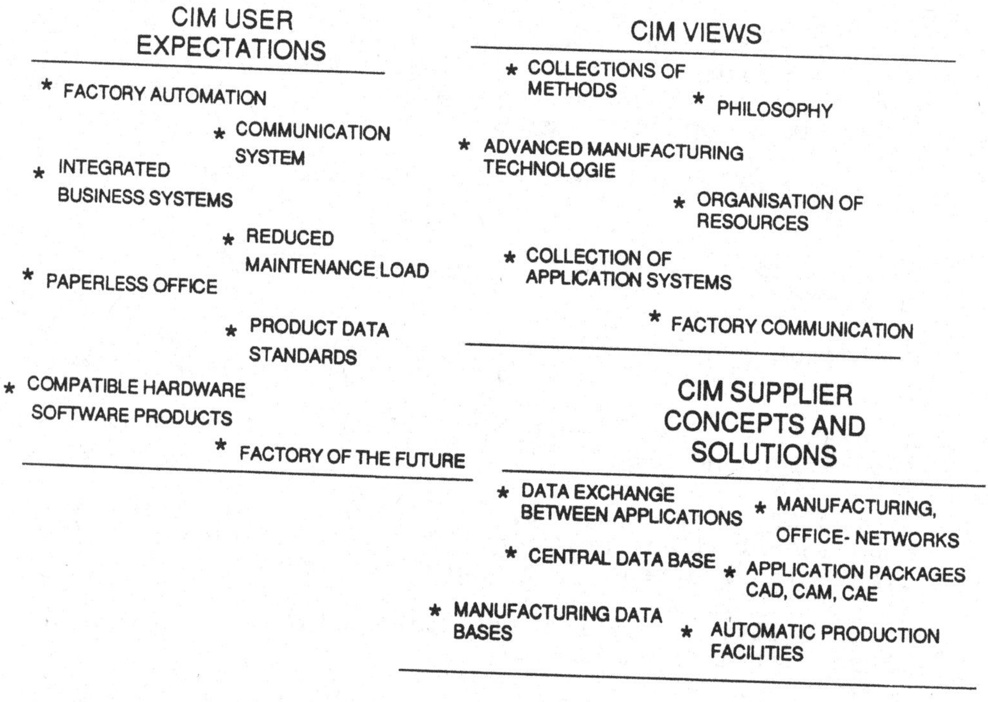

CIM USER EXPECTATIONS

* FACTORY AUTOMATION

    * COMMUNICATION SYSTEM

* INTEGRATED BUSINESS SYSTEMS

    * REDUCED MAINTENANCE LOAD

* PAPERLESS OFFICE

    * PRODUCT DATA STANDARDS

* COMPATIBLE HARDWARE SOFTWARE PRODUCTS

    * FACTORY OF THE FUTURE

CIM VIEWS

* COLLECTIONS OF METHODS
    * PHILOSOPHY

* ADVANCED MANUFACTURING TECHNOLOGIE

    * ORGANISATION OF RESOURCES

* COLLECTION OF APPLICATION SYSTEMS

    * FACTORY COMMUNICATION

CIM SUPPLIER CONCEPTS AND SOLUTIONS

* DATA EXCHANGE BETWEEN APPLICATIONS
* MANUFACTURING, OFFICE- NETWORKS

* CENTRAL DATA BASE
* APPLICATION PACKAGES CAD, CAM, CAE

* MANUFACTURING DATA BASES
* AUTOMATIC PRODUCTION FACILITIES

Figure 1-1: The Expectations on Integration

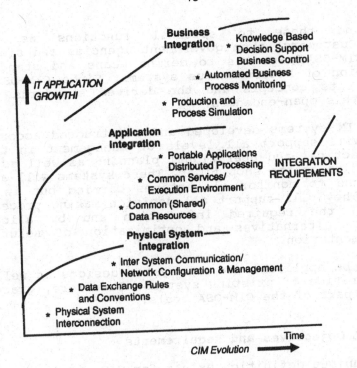

Figure 1-2: The Levels of Enterprise Integration

To solve the many problems of the manufacturing industry integration has to be done in more than one aspect. Figure 1-2 indicates three levels of integration which have been identified to guide the development of CIM-OSA. The **Physical System Integration** is mainly concerned with inter-system communication. CIM-OSA expects this level of integration to be provided by current Information Technology concepts and standards (e.g. OSI). CIM-OSA will use the relevant services as defined. CIM-OSA is concentrating on the other two levels of integration **Application Integration** and **Business Integration**. It will provide solutions for intra-system communication (**Application Integration**) and for enterprise requirement definition and CIM system design (**Business Integration**).

1.2 CIM-OSA Overview

1.2.1 Scope and Goal of CIM-OSA

The goal of CIM-OSA is to provide an Open System Architecture which will make the forthcoming permanent changes in the business environment manageable. Starting from the business needs, CIM-OSA will cover all aspects of the information required by all functions in a manufacturing enterprise. Therefore, it has to consider the internal relations and those to external functions as well (Suppliers, Customers, even government agencies and similar services). CIM-OSA also has to define means and standards for integration of heterogeneous systems. Since CIM-OSA is to be open, its concepts and the derived standards will provide for this open-endeness.

This means CIM systems developed and constructed according to CIM-OSA will support all levels of management in their strategic, tactical and operational planning as well as the direct operation at the shop floor. These systems will allow to control and to monitor all actions carried out in the enterprise. They will support all decision making processes by providing the required information and by allowing simulation of alternatives and optimization of solutions before implementation.

CIM-OSA will be applicable to new system designs as well as to the integration of existing systems. Therefore, graceful migration is part of the CIM-OSA goals.

1.2.2 CIM-OSA Objectives and Requirements

Although no unique definition exists for CIM, it is regarded as a strategic organisational concept for manufacturing industries where maximum use is made of information, supported by cost effective implementation of the capabilities of current and future Information Technologies.

CIM should and will provide to the industry opportunities to streamline production flows, to reduce lead times and to increase overall quality while adapting the enterprise fully to the needs of the market.

Adaptability and flexibility in a turbulent environment is a key issue. Obviously, the flexibility of the enterprise is dependent on and supported by the flexibility of its information system. However, there will be no general solution for all manufacturing industries let alone for all enterprises.

As an architecture CIM-OSA will guide CIM users in designing and implementing CIM systems by employing components which are developed according to CIM-OSA. CIM-OSA will also guide CIM vendors in developing marketable products which are implementable in CIM systems designed according to CIM-OSA.

CIM-OSA supports the gathering of user requirements for CIM systems by providing constructs for formulating these requirements.

CIM-OSA supports the creation of the CIM system description directly from the user requirements. From this system description an executable CIM system operation control will be derived.

The required system design process is supported by information technology. This ensures system consistency and basic optimization. Nevertheless, the total design process for the implemented CIM system still requires skilled human intervention for design choices of components and logical and physical grouping of those components for system optimization.

These design choices and optimization are a very important part of the creation of the CIM system. It is really this design process which yields the individual company competitiveness in the market place.

This leads to a certain number of requirements for the CIM systems and for the CIM-OSA Architecture:

o   For a given enterprise the CIM system implementation is to be ultimately described by a particular model which embodies all necessary knowledge of the enterprise in a form which can be used directly for the specification of an integrated set of electronic, mechanical, and Information Technology components necessary for effective realisation of the enterprise operations.

o   The resulting CIM system description has to be executable on Information Technology. This requires an system wide support system for CIM system design and operation.

o   Requirements for the CIM system have to expressible by the user using his terminology. These requirements have to be independent from implementation aspects such as the actual distribution, storage and processing of the information.

o   Integration has to be an on-going process rather than a one time effort. The level of integration should remain a managerial decision and should be changeable over time. Hence, one could find in some parts of a CIM enterprise, a set of tightly-coupled systems and elsewhere, a set of loosely coupled systems according to choices made by this particular enterprise.

o   Dynamic interconnecting of Information Technology based processes instead of permanently programmed sequences of activities.

o   Implementation of the multi-vendor systems both in terms of hardware and software and easy re-configurability.

Summarising the requirements for CIM-OSA:

CIM-OSA has to provide a widely accepted and well understood CIM system concept with a sufficient set of architectural constructs to structure the CIM system. Such a CIM system concept has to be based on an unambiguous and well accepted terminology. Such a concept will serve as a common technical base for CIM system implementors and CIM component and sub-system suppliers.

1.3 Content of CIM-OSA

Only a **CIM Reference Architecture** will provide a general framework which still allows individual companies to optimize their particular CIM architecture according to their own specific requirements.

The purpose of a CIM Reference Architecture is to define generic structures for the completely structured description of the enterprise as a SYSTEM. This description has to include the dynamic behaviour of its manufacturing processes, its information processes and its management processes. Specific emphasis has to be placed on the Information Technology support environments for system design, maintenance and operation. Only if all three are considered simultaneously will system consistency be achieved.

Within the AMICE project the CIM-OSA concept has been developed which provides such a Reference Architecture. Figure 1-3 shows a very general representation of the CIM-OSA modelling approach. The CIM-OSA Reference Architecture is the base from which CIM-OSA Particular Architectures can be instanciated. Particular Architectures provide a Frame for the modelling of particular enterprises. Filling this frame leads to the different particular models defined by CIM-OSA. The three directional processes refer to the internal structure of the Reference Architecture and how the different contents are created across the architecture.

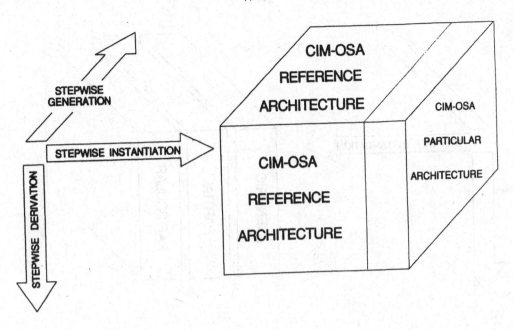

Figure 1-3: CIM-OSA Modelling Approach

1.3.1 The CIM-OSA Framework

The CIM-OSA Framework can be represented with different structures. Depending on the particular purpose of representation emphasis could be on its different levels of architectural genericity, different levels of enterprise and system modelling or different views of enterprise and system content. Figure 1-3 illustrates the overall framework of CIM-OSA.

1.3.1.1 CIM-OSA Architectural Levels

The CIM-OSA Framework has 3 levels of architectural genericity (Figure 1-4). The Reference Architecture is structured into 2 levels (**Generic Level** and **Partial Level**). These levels contain all the constructs required to gather the user requirements for his system operation and to translate these requirements into a consistent system description and implementation. The **Particular Level** is identical with the Particular Architecture. As such it contains the specific requirements for the specific enterprise operations and all specified, selected and implemented system components which satisfy these requirements.

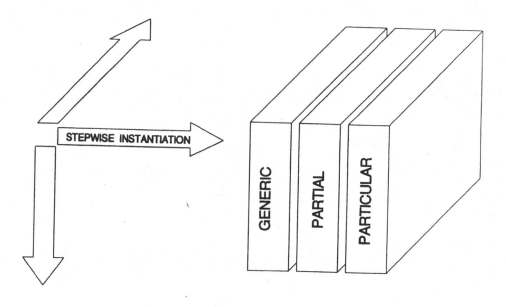

Figure 1-4: CIM-OSA Architectural Levels

1.3.1.2 CIM-OSA Modelling Levels

The 3 modelling levels of CIM-OSA (Figure 1-5) are concerned with the requirements on the **Requirements Definition Modelling level**, the system description on the **Implementation Description Modelling level** and with a logically, non-redundant representation of the requirements at the **Design Specification Modelling level**. This modelling level acts as an isolation between the user representation and the system representation on the levels above and below the intermediate one.

Each modelling level is comprised of its related constructs at the reference architectural levels and the resulting content at the Particular Architecture level.

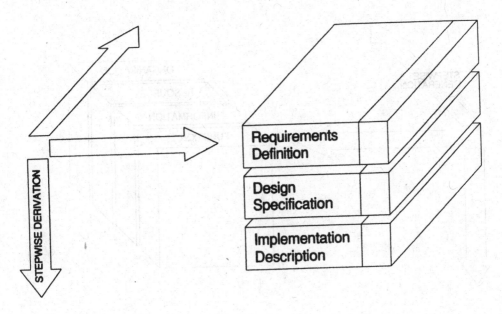

Figure 1-5: CIM-OSA Modelling Levels

1.3.1.3 CIM-OSA Views

4 different views (Figure 1-6) have been identified which allow to model the major aspects of the enterprise independent of each other. The **function view** is the representation of the enterprise operation in terms of a set of hierarchically structured business processes. Each business process is defined by its triggering events, the results it produces and by its explicit control flow description (its procedural rule set). The internal structure of a business process or the actions controlled by the procedural rule set may be either lower level business processes or executable enterprise activities.

The **information view** gathers all information defined and contained in the enterprise. These information is structured through a hierarchically defined set of information classes and through a set of schemata based on the 3 schema approach as defined by ISO. The **resource view** and the **organization view** contain all relevant information on enterprise resources and responsibilities in the enterprise. Both views are structured using the hierarchical concept of cells for grouping resources or organising responsibilities according to enterprise requirements.

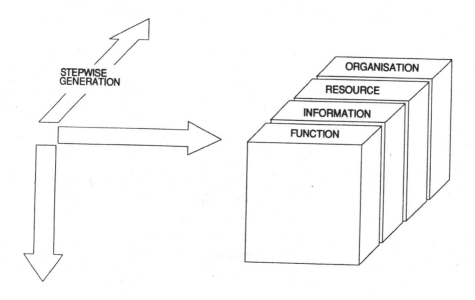

Figure 1-6: CIM-OSA Views

CIM-OSA considers the organization view of special importance. It allows to gather and structure the different responsibilities in the enterprise (for functions, information and resources). CIM-OSA provides a structuring concept which allows to describe the responsibilities in a multi-dimensional hierarchy.

It is through this representation of its responsibilities that CIM-OSA achieves the improved decision making process in the enterprise. And it is through this explicit organizational knowledge that the adaptability and flexibility of the enterprise is obtained.

Each of the 4 views is comprised of the related contents of all the architectural and modelling levels.

Figure 1-7 shows the CIM-OSA Framework resulting from the overlay of all architectural and modelling levels with all views. However, this representation of CIM-OSA is for CIM-OSA Architects rather than for CIM users.

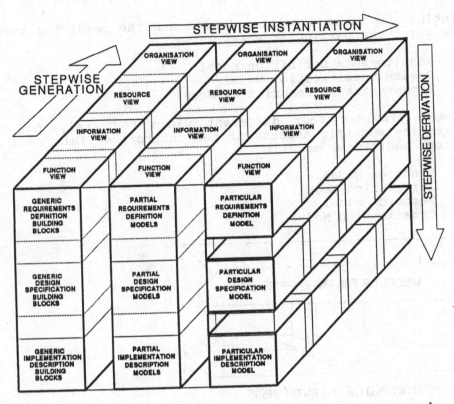

Figure 1-7: Overview of CIM-OSA Architectural Framework

1.3.1.4 The CIM-OSA Creation Process

CIM-OSA provides a set of guide-lines to create the different contents of the Particular Architecture from those of the Reference Architecture. To ease the definitions of these guide-lines the creation process has been decomposed into its 3 dimensions (see Figure 1-3). Instantiation, derivation and generation are applied between all the levels and views of the architecture. The creation process inside the Reference Architecture is controlled by the owners of the Reference Architecture. The process of creating a Particular Architecture is to be applied by the user of CIM-OSA himself. Therefore this process will be guided and supported significantly by Information Technology to assure the creation of consistent CIM system descriptions.

1.3.2 Main Components of CIM-OSA

CIM-OSA provides solutions for business integration and intra-system communication (see Figure 1-2). For enterprise requirements definition and CIM system design the CIM-OSA solution are three modelling levels and the resulting three models for the particular enterprise:

> Requirements Definition Model
> Design Specification Model
> Implementation Description Model

CIM-OSA provides four different views for analysing and optimizing specific aspects of the enterprise. This results in four additional models:

> Function Model
> Information Model
> Resource Model
> Organisation Model

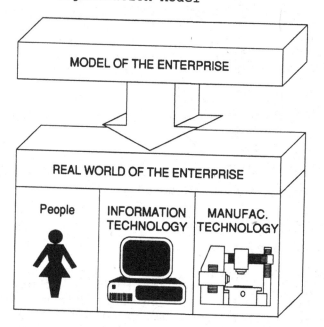

Figure 1-8: Implementation of CIM-OSA

Intra-system communication is achieved through the CIM-OSA Integrating Infrastructure. This Integrating Infrastructure supports system wide exchange of information for enterprise operation integration. It provides additional services supporting business integration (execution of the defined and designed CIM system - Run Time Support). These services will replace current DP based software application development by a user driven, requirement based Information Technology support system (Build Time Support).

Enterprise systems have to be implemented by employing People and using Manufacturing and Information Technology.

Figure 1-8 indicate the implementation of the CIM-OSA models, which contain all the enterprise requirements and the resulting designs, on the real world of people and technology components. Models and real world comprise the CIM system of the enterprise.

1.3.2.1 CIM-OSA Information Technology Components

CIM-OSA is based on the application of Information Technology to support design, maintenance and operation of CIM systems. This support is based on an Integrated Data Processing Environment (IDPE). It is this environment which provides the integration of heterogeneous Manufacturing and Information Technology and which allows for portability of application software across the heterogeneous physical world.

CIM-OSA defines specific environments as parts of the IDPE to separate and to structure the different tasks the Information Technology has to support (see Figure 1-9). For the creation process CIM-OSA provides a Build Time Support Environment to create and to maintain the Particular Architecture.

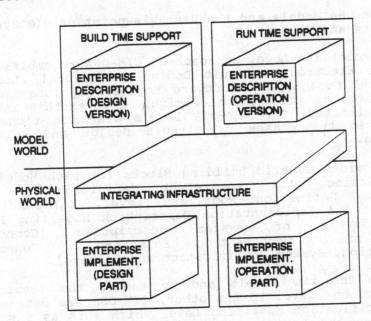

Figure 1-9: CIM-OSA Information Technology Environments

CIM-OSA provides a Run Time Support Environment for the enterprise operation and the execution of the content of the Particular Architecture. Both environments use for execution an Integrated Infrastructure (IIS) which provides specific Information Technology Services for the execution but more important provides for vendor independence and portability.

The CIM-OSA Integrated Infrastructure provides a set of services for system wide information exchange and operation support which are concerned with:

o   Communication:
         Communication Management
         System Wide Exchange
o   Information:
         System Wide Data
         Data Management
o   Front Ends:
         Human Front End
         Machine Front End
         Application Front End
o   Business Processes:
         Business Process Control
         Activity Control
         Resource Management

1.3.2.2 CIM-OSA Models and the User Viewpoint of CIM System Requirements and Design

The three Modelling Level approach of CIM-OSA resembles some analogy to Electronic Circuit Design (Functional, Logical and Physical Design) and Software Engineering (Requirement Analysis, Logical and Physical Design). However this analogy is rather limited. The CIM-OSA levels are much richer in content than the phases of Circuit Design and Software Engineering.

CIM-OSA provides Generic Building Blocks for each Modelling Level starting with requirement definitions at the Requirements Definition Modelling Level. CIM-OSA also contains in its Implementation Description Modelling Level several levels of system description (Component Specification, Component Selection, Component Implementation, System Qualification and Release).

To isolate the two levels and to reduce the impact of changes from one level to the other, CIM-OSA has defined an Design Specification Modelling Level which acts as a stable base between the business requirements definition and the system description.

In this role the Design Specification Modelling Level represents the optimized user requirements, taking into account all the enterprise business and system constraints. This optimization is carried out by systems organizers which optimize across the different user requirements from a global enterprise viewpoint in terms of business needs and system capabilities.

Figure 1-10 shows the content of the Particular Architecture as it applies to a specific enterprise. It shows the different CIM-OSA models and the user inputs provided at the different design phases. The **Requirements Definition Model** contains the enterprise business requirements. It is the domain of the Business User. The CIM user will define his requirements using the Reference Architecture constructs of the Requirements Definition Modelling Level. This will lead to the definition of sets of business processes and enterprise activities. These user requirements will be structured in the different views as indicated in Figure 1-10. Optimization of enterprise operation will start at this level. The content of the views will be evaluated according to user criteria (need of resources by different business processes, distribution of responsibility, etc.).

From the Enterprise Model an **Design Specification Model** is derived by considering overall enterprise system and operational constrains. These constrains together with removing redundancies and logically restructuring of the Enterprise Modelling Views leads to the Design Specification Modelling Views. Additional information will be added to the requirements like grouping of resources and of responsibilities. The Design Specification Model is the domain of the System Organizer.

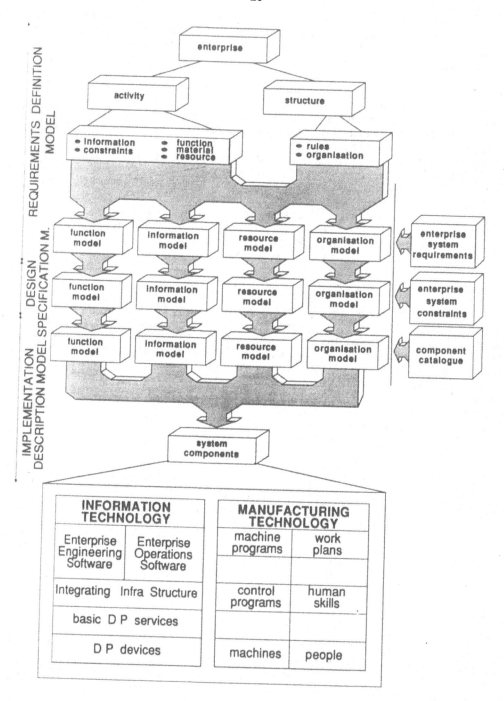

Figure 1-10: CIM-OSA Particular Architecture

Translating requirements into implemented solutions leads to the Implementation Modelling Level. The Implementation Model which contains the complete description of the enterprise system and operation is derived from the Design Specification Model in three phases:

o   specifying the CIM system components which will satisfy the defined requirements.
o   selecting real components from CIM component supplier catalogues or built according to the CIM-OSA specifications.
o   implement and validate the received components.

The Implementation Model is the domain of the System Implementor.

The completed system description and the real CIM system are released to the enterprise operation. The released model controls, via the IIS, the real CIM system which produces the real products of the enterprise.

1.4 Applying CIM-OSA

By analogy to the well known concept of product life cycle a CIM system life cycle has been defined in CIM-OSA. The basic Life Cycle consists of 4 phases; the first 3 phases are called **CIM-OSA Build Time** and the 4th phase is called **CIM-OSA Run Time**:

    System Requirement Specification
    System Design
    System Build and Release
    System Operation

Figure 1-11 illustrates the content of the different Life Cycle phases. At the requirement and design phase the business user (requirement definition) and CIM system designer (translation into system description) start with the content of the CIM-OSA Reference Architecture and create with the Build Time Support their part of the enterprise description (the Particular Architecture). The defined, specified, selected and built or bought CIM system components have to be implemented and released from the Build Time phases to the Run Time phase of the system life cycle. This release is done in parallel on the modelling level and on the physical level.

The released model is used to control the execution of the enterprise operation. Any modification occurring either in the modelling or in the physical world will be introduced again in the build time phase. This implies a complete separation of CIM system changes from its operation. All optimization, modifications, additions, maintenance at large will be done in an off-line mode using design models rather than operational models so easing the management of change.

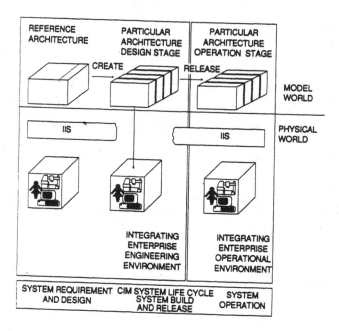

Figure 1-11: Applying CIM-OSA - the CIM System Life Cycle

1.5 CIM-OSA Relation to State of the Art

The relation of CIM-OSA to State of the Art exists in two different areas: in the CIM architecture area and in the area of Information Technology Standards.

The CIM-OSA concept is very different from any of the current efforts in CIM architecture in two aspects:

CIM-OSA starts its structuring approach from the requirements of business integration. It gathers the business requirements and derives from these requirements the relevant CIM system solution. In CIM-OSA this process of translation from requirements into consistent CIM system description is Information Technology supported.

Since CIM-OSA is to be applicable to all manufacturing industries and all types of enterprises only a reference framework can be defined with sufficient support to create enterprise specific architectures.

The major relation of CIM-OSA with efforts in standardization are in the CIM-OSA Integrated Infrastructure development work. The IIS services relate to on-going efforts in OSI, MAP and TOP and other relevant activities in distributed processing in ISO/IEC JC1 and ISO TC184. CIM-OSA will use standardized services like those defined in the OSI layers and will define complementary structures only where required.

The architectural work of CIM-OSA relates to the work on reference models in ISO TC184/SC5/WG1. In this area relevant inputs to standardization will be made.

1.6 Project Results and Status of CIM-OSA

1.6.1 Current Level of Validation and Applicability

In addition to the several reviews of the whole conceptual framework and its components, carried out by experts of the participating companies, the architecture was used for:

- applying the Requirements Definition Model in 4 case studies in the aerospace, automotive and electronics industry;

- applying the IDPE (Integrated Data Processing Environment) model on special scenarios;

- developing a CIM-OSA concept demonstration on a workstation. This demonstration deserves special attention since, in addition to its obvious validation role, it constitutes an excellent awareness tool for explaining in a dynamic way the architectural concepts. Moreover, one is able to see how the architecture could be used in designing CIM systems.

1.6.2 Current Level of Involvement in Standardization

The AMICE project is involved in national and international standards organizations through its members who are active participants in the relevant standardization bodies. Nevertheless through these people the CIM-OSA concepts have been actively presented and are considered in several Committees and Working Groups as major contribution to the subject of Reference Models and Architecture in the CIM area.

Specific Contributions have been made to:

ISO TC184/SC5/WG1

German DIN / KCIM group and VDMA / NAM 96.5

1.6.3 Future Contributions to CIM-OSA

The AMICE project has defined and started to validate the major concepts of CIM-OSA. The concepts of Generic Building Blocks, the creation of a Particular Architecture from a Reference Architecture, the three Modelling Levels, the four Views and last but not least the Integrating Infrastructure have been developed to a point of relative good overall consistency.

Contributions in the architectural areas have to be made by the development team itself. However it could be envisaged that in the near future other organizations could contribute to areas like partial models, tools and even new building block definitions.

1.7 Benefits of CIM-OSA

CIM-OSA will improve the user enterprise operation in two main areas:

o   the ability to adapt itself in 'real time' to changes in the market and in the external environment in general

o   the efficiency in using its assets.

These major benefits are achieved through the well defined CIM system design and (even more important) maintenance process; through the drastically improved availability of information - the improved decision making processes and through the ability to adapt and optimize the enterprise operation dynamically.

However, CIM-OSA will improve the supplier enterprise operation as well.

o   the standardization of CIM systems will increase the market volume for CIM system components drastically

o   the improved acceptance of CIM systems will make introduction of new and advanced features of Information Technology and Manufacturing Technology much more easy.

2. Project Perspective

A perspective on AMICE start-up, evolution and possible results is given by a four step scenario. The four steps, illustrate in chronological order the following situations:

1.   Before AMICE
2.   Starting AMICE
3.   AMICE Project
4.   After AMICE

illustrated in Figures 2-1 to 2-4

2.1 Before AMICE

The first situation (Figure 2-1) illustrates the context in which a need for a reference CIM Architecture arose.

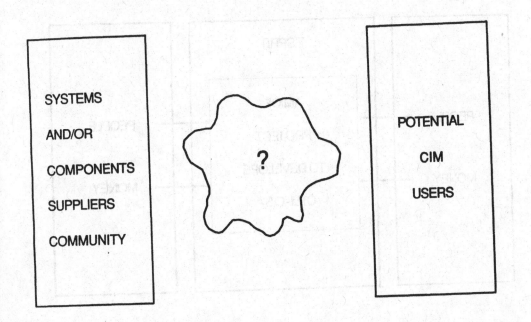

Figure 2-1: Before AMICE

The two communities of CIM system implementors and CIM system component suppliers are facing different aspects of what will be recognized to be a common problem.

o   Industries with a need of improvement of productivity and flexibility and a vague not well defined set of needs.

o   Suppliers of components for factory automation with a
     feeling about an enormous potential market but with
     very vague set of requirements and hazardous forecast
     of the size and growth rates of the different market
     segments.

This situation is made more problematical by the lack of a
common language between the individual members of the two
communities.

2.2 Starting AMICE

In this context the ESPRIT effort promoted and supported by
the C.E.C. offers a good framework in which to start
preparing a common background for the classification of what
C.I.M. could mean in terms of components, architecture,
applicability, cost/performance etc.

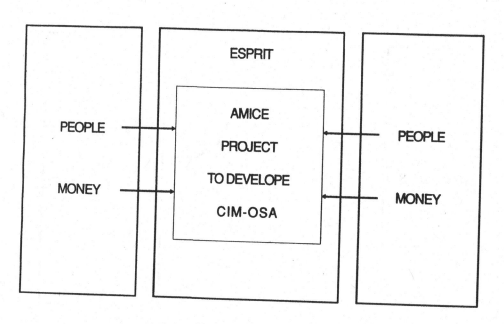

Figure 2-2: Starting AMICE

The aggregation of several groups proposing to address the
topic of CIM architecture from different points of view
resulted in the AMICE Consortium generating a proposal for
the CIM OSA Project. In this project (Figure 2-2) the major
European Industries both from the Suppliers and User
Communities were brought together to share financial
resources, know-how and people with the aim of generating a
reference CIM architecture.

2.3 The AMICE Project

The CIM OSA Project (Figure 2-3) deals with the definition of a general Open Systems Architecture (CIM-OSA).

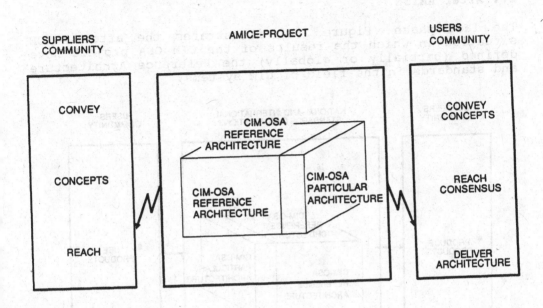

Figure 2-3: AMICE Project

Industries participating in the project get back, via their participation, a set of basic concepts and a common understanding of the terms of the problem, which will be more detailed and refined as the project proceeds. At the end of AMICE the whole set of reference and structured models will be released in the different contexts.

In the System Suppliers Community these models will be the reference for designing and producing global systems or components for the implementation of real CIM Systems.

In the Users Community those models will be used as reference to create the equivalent personalized models needed in a particular environment and in this way define precise requirements for the required CIM system and its individual components.

In the standardisation context at large, these models and their relations will be proposed as possible standards.

The common understanding generated during the previous
phases of CIM-OSA Project will help to generate consensus in
these contexts.

2.4 After AMICE

The last phase (Figure 2-4) illustrates the after AMICE
situation in which the results of the CIM OSA project have
defined (partially or globally) the Reference Architecture
and standards in the field of CIM systems.

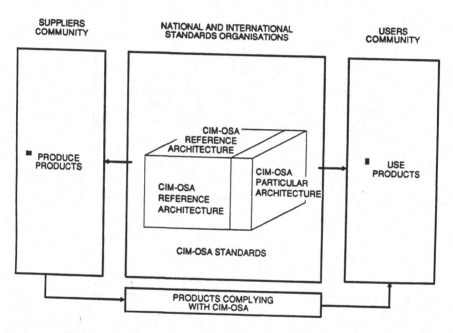

Figure 2-4: After AMICE

Starting from these standards the different suppliers can
produce products complying with CIM-OSA. Depending on their
strategies these products may be either general (in terms of
tools and architecture), or more specialized CIM systems for
given types of industries, or single building blocks (parts
of a CIM system) coherent with standards and agreed models.

The user community will be able to take advantage of a well
understood mechanism for defining the model of a specific
enterprise and to derive from that the design for the
specific CIM system needed. There will also be a competitive
marketplace from which to buy integrated systems or single
building blocks to be integrated in a customized way.

2.5 List of Participating Members

(* = Subcontractor)

Project Membership - Definition Phase Contract

Company	Name
AEG AKTIENGESELLSCHAFT	J. Beyer
	W. Blau
	M. Klittich
	W. Seifert
AEROSPATIALE	C. Acker
	J. Audy
	D. Claude
	B. Chiavassa
	R. Gaches
	P. Marechal
	G. Still
ALCATEL NV	P. Dix-Neuf
	G. Dureau
	A. Leffi
	J. Schoemacher
APT NEDERLAND B.V.	A. Devolder
	M. Katz
	J. Van Boven
	F. Van De Pijpekamp
	R. Van Den Dam
	J. Vlietstra
	D. Zoetekouw
BRITISH AEROSPACE plc.	G. Beadle
	G. Bishop
	B. Jackson
	R. Jordan
	R. Langhorne
	H. Mason
	M. Stenhouse
BULL S.A.	F. de Belenet
	J. Gimza
	M. Gougeon
	C. Guillier
	R. Lavie
	H. Posingies
	D. Ruesch
CAP INDUSTRIES (*)	I. Bays
	P. Cheshire
	K. Farman

CAP GEMINI SESA Belgium	D. Beeckman A. Bodart P. Daoust D. Deschamps M. Dessaintes J. Dorlhac R. De Gobert P. De Swert D. Fontaine J. Huysentruyt B. Lorimy R. Masgnaux J. Pedron
DIGITAL EQUIPMENT GmbH	G. Barta A. Bauer B. Bouyer U. Brunet A. Cote J. Gemsjaeger O. Jaervinnen D. Lane
DORNIER Luftfahrt GmbH	A. Harter O. Hasenfuss A. Huber N. Jurgen R. Kurz J. Nagel E. Sock H. Stephan
FIAT S.p.A.	V. Calamani E. Ceroni M. Mollo F. Naccari
GEC Electrical Projects Ltd.	D. Beaumont J. Beeston J. Fowle L. Frost R. Howie C. Manton A. Mistry C. Silvestro P. Warneck R. Watson
HEWLETT PACKARD FRANCE	J. Julia D. Pothier B. Querenet P. Viollet

IBM DEUTSCHLAND GmbH	H. Jorysz H. Kittel K. Kosanke R. Panse K. Rittmann P. Stecher E. Stotko M. Zelm
INRIA- LORRAINE (*)	J. Proth I. Roche F. Vernadat
INTERNATIONAL COMPUTERS Ltd.	T. Addison J. Kenny A. Lucas-Smith S. Ottley R. Rowley P. Russell
ITALSIEL	M. Arman F. Basso C. Bertusi M. Bonfadini G. Caldiera S. Rabatti B. Scialpi M. Taborelli R. Tansini
N.V. MBLE S.A. Philips	J. De Smet J. Emond N. Hecque T. Hermans G. Kaashoek R. Kommeren G. Marechal J. Matthys K. Metzger P. Mortier F. Ponsaert M. Schayes M. Staels J. Van Den Hanenberg

PROCOS A/S	P. Andersson
	A. Bonnevie
	C. Gry
	T. Jacobsen
	J. Jorgensen
	C. Krishnaswamy
	J. Langeland-Knudsen
	C. Lassen
	S. Moss
	T. Norup Pedersen
S.E.I.A.F. SPA	A. Asogna
	M. Busatti
	P. Chiabra
	B. Circe
	G. Cosmai
	U. Cugini
	R. De Grandi
	R. Ferrari
	R. Manara
	P. Murchio
	A. Passarelli
	G. Romano
	M. Tomijanivich
SIEMENS AKTIENGESELLSCHAFT	N. Haberkorn
	H. Koenig
	N. Luetkemeyer
	R. Meier
	N. Tran-Binh
	U. von Lippe
	M. Wieck
VOLKSWAGEN AG	A. Mund
	K. Pasemann
	G. Teunis
WZL AACHEN UNIVERSITY	G. Abolins
	M. Ahmadian
	T. Brachtendorf
	B. Dahl
	U. Dern
	A. Friedrich
	G. Goedecke
	J. Kimmelmann
	T. Klevers
	N. Lange
	G. Müller
	R. Neitzel
	G. Rothenbücher
	W. Ruehle
	J. Schütt
	E. Zahn

3. Introduction to CIM-OSA

The goal of CIM-OSA (Open System Architecture for CIM) is to enable the enterprise to perform its business in a real time adaptive mode. This goal will be reached by supporting operational flexibility and by supporting multi-disciplinary information (knowledge) integration and system integration. As an architecture CIM-OSA provides a framework which guides CIM users and CIM vendors. It also provides architectural constructs for the structured description of business requirements and for CIM system implementations.

The application of CIM-OSA results in a complete description of the enterprise which is stored on and manipulated by the relevant information technology base of the enterprise.

Many different representations of the manufacturing enterprise content and structure are required to satisfy the needs of the different users of such an architecture. CIM-OSA provides the necessary constructs to enable these multiple representations.

CIM-OSA provides a descriptive rather than a prescriptive methodology. It does not provide a standard architecture to be used by the whole manufacturing industry but rather a Reference Architecture from which Particular Architectures can be derived. Such Particular Architectures will fulfil the needs of particular enterprises.

To accomplish its goal CIM-OSA brings together a number of architectural principles and employs several structuring concepts.

3.1 Architectural Principles

The architectural principles used in CIM-OSA are as follows:

- Abstraction

- Modularity
    - Genericity and Instantiation
    - Modelling and Derivation
    - Views and Generation

- Open-endedness

- Isolation of User Requirements from System Implementation

3.2 Structuring Concepts

In addition four structuring concepts have been defined

- Descriptive Languages
  - Business descriptive language
  - System descriptive language
  - Computer supported translation from business descriptive language into system descriptive language

- Separation of Function and Control

- Generic Services and Protocols:
  Computer supported Design, Implementation and Execution of CIM Models

- System Life Cycle

These principles and concepts really set CIM-OSA apart from previous work in the area of Computer Integrated Manufacturing. The concepts themselves are known and have previously been applied separately in Manufacturing Technology and in Information Technology. However, their systematic and combined application is a significant step in the development of Computer Integrated Manufacturing.

3.3 Relation of CIM-OSA to the Real World

CIM-OSA provides an architecture to describe the real world of the manufacturing enterprise. This description is used to control the enterprise operation and to plan, design and optimise updates of the real operation environment.

CIM-OSA also provides an Information Technology based Integrating Infrastructure which provides for portability of computer applications, enables system wide information exchange and supports multi-vendors hardware and software. This Integrating Infrastructure is used during both Build Time and Run Time of CIM systems. Figure 3-1 shows the two environments which support Build Time (design phase) and Run Time (operational phase). Each environment is Information Technology supported and uses its related resources (people, equipment, hardware and software tools).

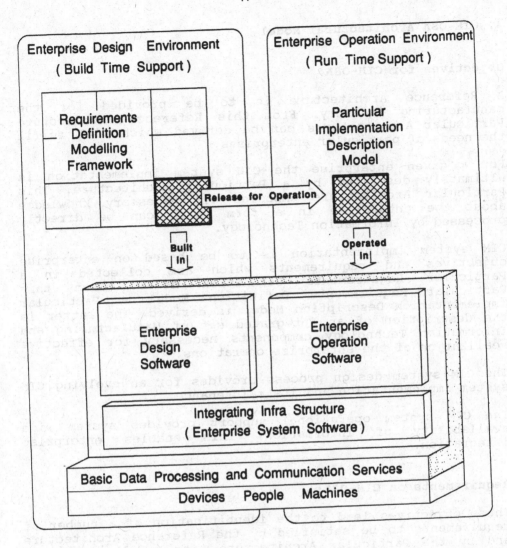

Figure 3-1: Role of CIM-OSA

4. CIM-OSA Architectural Model

Objectives for CIM-OSA:

A Reference Architecture is to be provided for the manufacturing industry. From this Reference Architecture Particular Architectures can be derived which will fulfil the needs of particular enterprises.

For a given enterprise the CIM system implementation is ultimately described by a Particular Architecture. This Particular Architecture embodies all necessary knowledge about the enterprise in a form which can be directly processed by Information Technology.

CIM system implementation is to be based on enterprise objectives and requirements which are collected in a Particular Requirements Definition Model. From this Particular Requirements Definition Model a Particular Implementation Description Model is derived. The latter is the description of an integrated set of Manufacturing and Information Technology components necessary for effective realization of the enterprise operations.

The CIM system design process provides for an evolving CIM system implementation and its maintenance.

The CIM system operational support provides system wide availability of information. This enables enterprise integration.

Requirements on CIM-OSA:

These objectives lead to the identification of a number of requirements to be satisfied by the Reference Architecture and by the Particular Architecture, its models and their derivations:

o   The models have to be derived and optimised for a particular enterprise according to a common reference framework.

o   The models have to reflect clearly the established enterprise decision making, its organisation, its activities, its business processes, its information interchange and its material flows, in a form suitable for translation into an actual and processable implementation.

o   The models have to be amenable to flexible modification, so as to reflect the changing enterprise environment, constraints and operations, and in particular to be capable of reflecting system implementations which are built in an evolutionary manner.

o   The models and their supporting guide-lines have to guide the user in the design, implementation and operation phases of such systems in a wide range of manufacturing industries.

o   The Reference Architecture and its supporting guide-lines have to guide the vendor in the design, implementation and marketing of such systems and system components.

o   Sufficient system support has to be made available to assure overall model and system consistency. This design support system has to relate new designs or modification of existing designs to the existing description of the enterprise CIM system and to provide design choices for new system components.

o   The CIM system operational support has to provide the integrating mechanism between the different enterprise parts. **Enterprise wide information interchange.**

User Design Phases of a Particular Architecture using CIM-OSA:

These needs presuppose an architectural design which can be arrived at in three distinct, but integrated, phases.

1.   To support the **capture of the enterprise's requirements** using a mapping against a common, neutral, supporting reference framework to achieve a consistent set of requirements (this process is termed 'instantiation').

2.   To **organize the captured requirements** in a form in which they can be realized by a **controlled set of Information Technology applications** (we have called this process 'derivation').

3.   To **support the analysis and synthesis of specific aspects** (View's) of the enterprise (this process is called generation).

The resultant Particular system description must be **modular** in nature. This modularity is the key to achieve flexibility and identify standards.

4.1 Architectural Framework of CIM-OSA

The need for modelling the enterprise and its associated CIM system in a coherent way has generated a modelling approach based on a Reference Architecture from which Particular Architectures can be developed. Applying the architectural principle of modularity leads to a three dimensional structure with three orthogonal axes (see Figure 4-1 left side).

On the **instantiation** axis different levels of genericity are defined which allow the CIM user to select building blocks to meet particular instances of his design needs. These needs start with user requirement definition and end with CIM system implementation. The **derivation** axis identifies the different modelling areas which are to be addressed by the enterprise when developing its own CIM system. Different views of specific enterprise aspects are identified on the **generation** axis (see Figure 4-2 for further details).

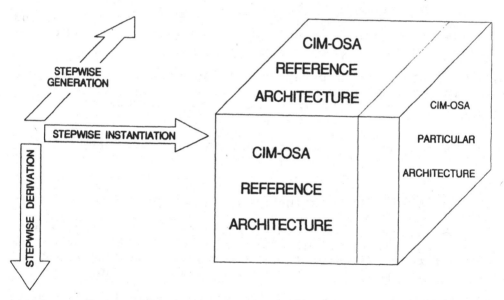

Figure 4-1: Modelling Approach

Figure 4-1 (right side) shows the volume generated by the three axes. This volume is divided into two parts the CIM-OSA Reference Architecture and the CIM-OSA Particular Architecture. The CIM-OSA Reference Architecture contains the whole set of architectural constructs required to describe the requirements of and the solutions for any particular enterprise. The enterprise specific requirements and realized solutions are captured in the CIM-OSA Particular Architecture.

The Reference Architecture consists of a catalogue containing the formal descriptions of constructs which are a synthesis of the generic characteristics of any manufacturing enterprise. These generic constructs do not imply any predefined, rigid form of enterprise structure, but instead provide the means by which such structure can be expressed in a common and consistent manner.

Therefore, CIM-OSA does not prescribe a systems architecture which is identical for every enterprise. CIM-OSA only provides the framework from which particular structures can be derived. Each Particular Architecture can be defined to fulfil the needs of the particular enterprise. CIM-OSA even allows optimising over time (CIM system maintenance).

CIM-OSA provides means for representations of constructs for modelling of user requirements, system specifications, addressing specific aspects of the enterprise (Function, Information, Resource, Organisation).

The **CIM-OSA Framework** is summarized in Figure 4-2. A 3x3x4 framework has been proposed. This framework also contains the guide-lines (processes) for instantiation, derivation and generation needed both in the generic context of a CIM-OSA reference and standardisation framework, and in the specific context of a particular enterprise, planning to define and implement its own CIM system.

Three levels of **Genericity** have been depicted by three vertical columns, and three levels of **Modelling** by horizontal sub-division of those columns. Four different **Views** extend this two-dimensional framework into a three dimensional one.

The three dimensions of CIM-OSA indicated in Figure 4-1 by the three arrows are different in nature for the CIM-OSA Reference Architecture and the CIM-OSA Particular Architecture.

The CIM user in his task of designing his CIM-OSA Particular Architecture will employ the stepwise Instantiation using relevant constructs from the Reference Architecture and will also use stepwise derivation and generation only inside the CIM-OSA Particular Architecture.

The three aspects of instantiation, derivation and generation within the Reference Architecture may come in the future under the control of standardisation bodies. However, users may create non-standard Partial Models for their own use employing all or some of the three aspects.

A strong implicit linkage (the derivation process) exists between the Requirements Definition Modelling constructs and the Implementation Description Modelling constructs to ensure realizations of the Requirements Definition Modelling constructs by CIM vendors. Thus there will be a fair chance that system components required will already exist in the market place.

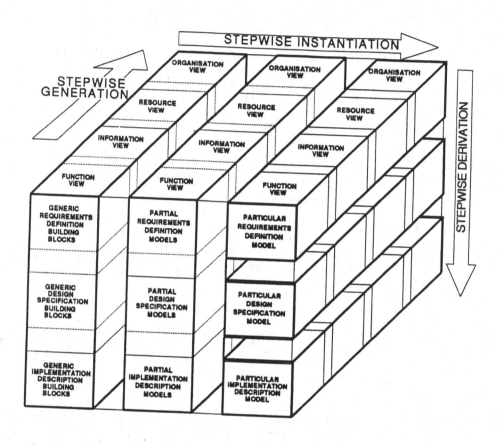

CIM-OSA Framework

Figure 4-2: Overview of Architectural Framework

All elements of the CIM-OSA Framework are described in more detail in the following sections:

4.1.1 Levels of Genericity and Stepwise Instantiation

According to its architectural principle (the generic approach) CIM-OSA has defined three levels of genericity ranging from the purely generic to the highly particular. In Figure 4-3 the shaded Generic Level indicates that each level of genericity contains an internal structure consisting of three modelling areas and four Views.

The **CIM-OSA Reference Architecture** contains the Generic and Partial Level of genericity whilst, the **CIM-OSA Particular Architecture** contains the Particular Level.

The **Generic Level** is a reference catalogue of basic CIM-OSA architectural constructs (building blocks) for components, constraints, rules, terms, service functions and protocols. Constructs described at this level have the widest application in CIM.

The **Partial Level** is concerned with sets of partially instantiated models applicable to a particular category of manufacturing enterprises. Such a partial instantiation will consist of typical structures for a variety of categories like industry-sector types (such as aerospace, automotive, electronics, etc.,) company size, national variations, etc. Partial Models may also be defined in a hierarchy as indicated in Figure 4-4; a set of Partial Models 'Automotive Suppliers' may be partially instantiated in a further subset according to enterprise size and even in a further subset according to type of business.

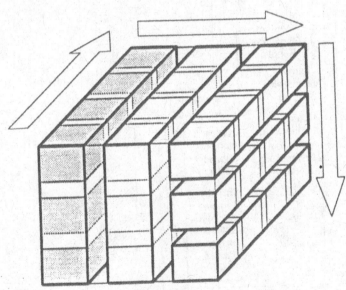

Figure 4-3: Levels of Genericity

Requirements for these structures will grow with time. Therefore, the Partial Level is considered to be an open set. This set will be populated according to the needs of standardisation bodies, industry offerings and even internal work in particular enterprises.

The Partial Models are the prime means by which CIM-OSA encapsulates industry requirements, and provides a more realistic and usable tool for instantiating CIM-OSA for a particular enterprise.

The Partial Level improves the economy of the CIM system design process by providing architectural constructs (Partial Models) applicable to more specific but still generic areas of an enterprise. Therefore, Partial Models are macro constructs generated from the basic building blocks of the Generic Level. This partially-instantiated set of Partial Models is also a reference catalogue.

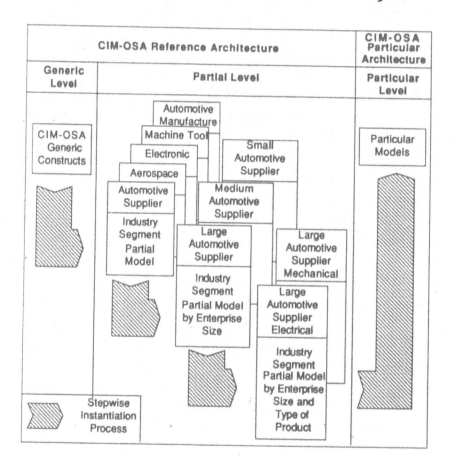

Figure 4-4: Partial Level

The **Particular Level** is entirely concerned with one particular enterprise. For such an enterprise the CIM system implementation has to be described by a Particular Architecture. This architecture embodies all necessary knowledge of the enterprise in a form which can be used directly for the specification of an integrated set of Manufacturing and Information Technology components. These components comprise the operational system which satisfies the business requirements of that particular enterprise.

The Particular Level can be instantiated either directly from the Generic Level and/or from the Partial Level (see also Figure 4-4).

This **stepwise Instantiation process** permits the orderly movement from a more generic level to a more Particular Level. A number of steps performed in the correct order permit movement from generic, abstract constructs to completely determined particular systems (see Figure 4-5).

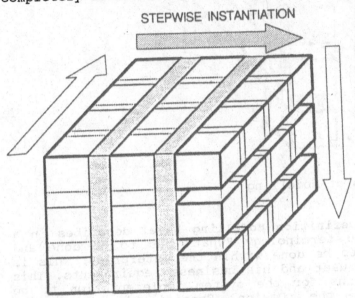

Figure 4-5: Stepwise Instantiation

Instantiation itself is controlled by a set of guide-lines which defines the process steps, constrains the process and ensures it is applied in a consistent manner.

4.1.2 Levels of Modelling and Stepwise Derivation

In CIM-OSA, three main Modelling Levels (**Requirements Definition, Design Specification** and **Implementation Description**) have been defined. These three Modelling Levels represent three different stages during the continuous evolution of a Particular Architecture.

In Figure 4-6 the shaded Requirements Definition Modelling Level indicates that each Modelling Level contains an internal structure consisting of three areas of genericity and four Views.

Each of the Modelling Levels is based on a set of reference constructs and is supported by a design methodology.

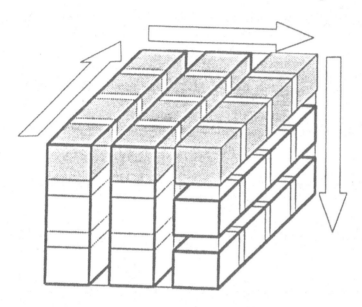

Figure 4-6: Levels of Modelling

The **Requirements Definition Modelling Level** describes in a business sense and terminology "what" has to be done and "how" things are to be done within the enterprise. This is the domain of the user and his business requirements. This still leaves options for the system implementation to be chosen at both the Design Specification and the Implementation Description Modelling Level.

Example: At the Requirements Definition Modelling Level the requirement is for automated machining of parts, leaving decisions on the type of machines for the two other Modelling Levels.

The **Implementation Description Modelling Level** specifies an integrated set of components necessary for effective realization of the enterprise operations. This is the domain of the implementor and his system implementation.

The CIM-OSA Implementation Description Modelling building blocks are directly related to those provided for the Requirements Definition Modelling Level and for the Design Specification Modelling Level. Thus there will be a fair chance that system components required will already exist in the market place. For any that do not there will exist a CIM-OSA specification which then can easily be implemented.

The **Design Specification Modelling Level** structures and optimises the business requirements defined by the multiplicity of users according to overall business and system constraints. This is the domain of the system organizer and his enterprise organisation.

Example: Considering the available Manufacturing Technology and economical aspects, the decision will be made at this Modelling Level to use milling for the automated machining of parts.

The Design Specification Modelling Level bridges between the two other levels (from information requirements as described in the Requirements Definition Model to the processing of data by Information Technology).

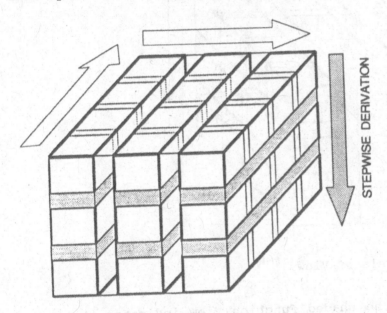

Figure 4-7: Stepwise Derivation Process

The **stepwise Derivation process** (see Figure 4-7) provides an orderly derivation of enterprise implementation from enterprise requirements. This process employs Design Specification Views to restructure the requirements from the users definition into more system related specification.

Derivation is the translation from a business description language into a system description language. Derivation itself is controlled by a set of guide-lines which defines steps in the process, constrains the process and ensures it is applied in a consistent manner.

The derivation process is of a different nature for the different levels of genericity (see above).

4.1.3 Levels of Views and Stepwise Generation

CIM-OSA defines the four different **Views** which are needed to fully model specific aspects of the enterprise.

These Views are concerned with enterprise **Function**, its **Information**, its **Resources** and its **Organisation**.

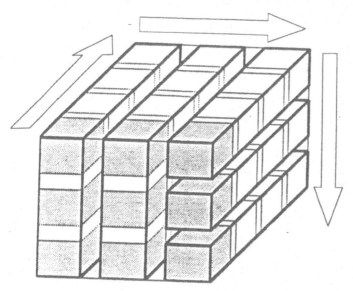

Figure 4-8: Levels of Views

In Figure 4-8 the shaded Function View indicates that each View contains an internal structure consisting of three generic and three modelling areas.

The **Function View** describes the functional structure required to satisfy the objectives of the enterprise and the related control structure i.e. the rules which define the control sequences, or flow of action within the enterprise and the principles of underlying business processes.

The **Information View** describes the information required by each function (at the Requirements Definition Modelling Level, this is the business user's view of information rather than the DP view).

The **Resource View** describes the resources and their relationship to functional and control structures, and organisational structures.

The **Organisation View** is the description of the enterprise organisational structures i.e. the responsibilities assigned to individuals for functional and control structures, information and resources.

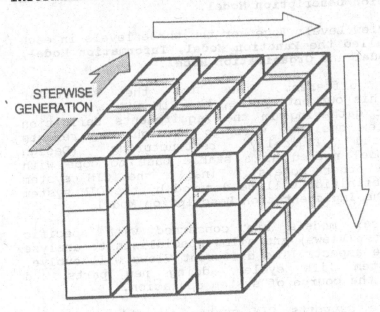

Figure 4-9: Stepwise Generation Process

The **stepwise Generation Process** (see Figure 4-9) starts from the requirement gathering and its content in terms of function requirements and generates all the Views (Function, Information, Resource and Organisation) in an iterative optimisation manner.

Generation itself is controlled by a set of guide-lines which defines the process steps, constrains the process and ensures it is applied in a consistent manner.

4.2 CIM-OSA Models

The CIM-OSA Reference Architecture defines all the constructs for instantiation of a Particular Architecture (Building Blocks and Partial Models). Grouping of these constructs exist but they are more of a catalogue type rather than a model.

At the Particular Architecture Level sets' of Views are grouped to represent different models within the Particular Architecture for an enterprise. There are two groups of models:

o   Models at Modelling Level: Together the four Views on each Modelling Level are called the **Requirements Definition Model, Design Specification Model** and **Implementation Description Model.**

o   Models at View Level: Together the three levels in each View are called the **Function Model, Information Model, Resource Model** and **Organisation Model.**

Developing the different Views for the Particular Architecture of his own enterprise, the CIM user will start with requirement gathering in the Requirements Definition Model. The system designer will go through requirements optimisation and logically restructuring (Design Specification Model needed as a stable base to cope with changes in the other models). Finally the CIM system implementation definition will be derived by the CIM system implementor in the Implementation Description Model.

The four vertical models are concerned with specific enterprise aspects (Views) and allow specialists to analyse and improve these aspects. The different Views will evolve, during the system life cycle, adding new parts and modifications in the course of system operation.

CIM-OSA therefore supports CIM system iterations (system maintenance) through its models. This recognizes the very important aspect of system modifications and enhancements being a major aspect of CIM system development. However, CIM-OSA in its CIM system life cycle considers system maintenance to be of the same nature as system design.

4.3 CIM-OSA Relation to State of the Art

The most important papers and reports related to CIM Architectures have been analyzed and compared with the CIM-OSA concept according to a defined set of evaluation criteria.

State of the Art material relating to the following projects was analysed:

-   ICAM project 1105: Conceptional Design for Computer Integrated Manufacturing
-   CAM-I DPMM: Discrete Parts Manufacturing Model
-   NBS AMRF: Automated Manufacturing Research Facility
-   ISO TC 184/SC5/WG1 N51: Ottawa Report on Reference Models for Manufacturing Standards

- ESPRIT Pilot Project 34: Design Rules for Computer Integrated Manufacturing Systems
- ANSA: Advanced Networked System Architecture

Evaluation Criteria for State of the Art

To compare CIM-OSA with the State of the Art material the following evaluation criteria have been applied.

- Scope/Architectural Goals
- Industrial Environment (Industry Type) addressed
- Enterprise Functions covered
- Architectural Models provided
- Methodology and Tools applied

Comparison between State of the Art and CIM-OSA

The results of this evaluation are summarized in the table below:

	State of the Art	CIM-OSA
Scope	architecture/model for particular unique industrial environment	Reference Architecture for all industrial environments and guidelines for CIM product development
Environment	discrete parts manufacturing with emphasis on mechanical parts and aerospace manufacturing	discrete part manufacturing (electrical, electronic, mechanical) and CIM vendors (machine tool and IT industry)
Functions	focus on manufacturing functions, complementary functions taken into account	all functions in a manufacturing enterprise
Models	hierarchical/top down decomposition of functions and data (control structure and management)	reference catalogue for enterprise, design and implementation modelling
Methodology	free form textual description and graphs/flow charts DVM: Data Vector Modelling IDEF - ICAM Definition based on SADT, ERA	System design using finite set of generic building blocks for computer supported modelling and computer supported enterprise operation

This evaluation indicates the difference in scope and content of CIM-OSA compared with the State of the Art material analyzed. CIM-OSA is not a Particular Architecture but a Reference Architecture which provides computerized support for the development of Particular Architectures for individual enterprises.

CIM-OSA will support the individual business user in defining and developing his own models as part of an overall Requirements Definition Model. In addition CIM-OSA will support the enterprise operation by translating the user requirements into a description of CIM system components (resources and executable Information Technology applications).

4.4 Architecture Summary

Today the manufacturing industry is faced with a rapidly changing Business Environment. Varying market demands require frequent operational and organisational changes in the individual enterprise.

CIM-OSA therefore enables the user to describe his enterprise from two distinct standpoints. That of the Business Environment as seen by the business user, and that of the equivalent Physical Environment - the Manufacturing and Information Technology implemented in the enterprise. CIM-OSA facilitates the collection of the business requirements of the enterprise in an Requirements Definition Model. These requirements are translated into a description of the implemented CIM system - the Implementation Description Model. To derive this system description all specific constraints of the particular enterprise are taken into account in the Design Specification Model. CIM-OSA provides a creation process (instantiation, derivation, generation) which allows a guided translation from the enterprise requirements to the system implementation.

CIM-OSA provides a Reference Architecture as a framework for the specific description of a particular enterprise. The architectural constructs of CIM-OSA will guide the CIM user in the design process to obtain a consistent system description. These construct will also guide the CIM supplier to develop, produce and market products which will fit the defined user requirements.

The architectural constructs provided for the description can be viewed as a description language for the manufacturing enterprise which constitutes a completely new method for application program development in the CIM area. A method which allows the end user to define, to design, to implement and to execute the business processes according to his needs. The architecture also defines the necessary support environment for development and execution.

The following Chapter will concentrate on the modelling representation of CIM-OSA. This representation is considered to be the most important one for the use of CIM-OSA

5. The CIM-OSA Modelling Levels

CIM-OSA provides three Modelling Levels to model enterprise requirements (Requirements Definition Modelling Level), system optimisation (Design Specification Modelling Level) and system implementation (Implementation Description Modelling Level). To provide decision criteria, user inputs have to be provided at each CIM system design stage (the 3 Modelling Levels).

The Requirements Definition Model contains a number of fundamental business aspects which are expressed in Views (function, rules, constraints, information/material, resources and organisation). All of these aspects must be accurately reflected in the Implementation Description Model. Figure 5-1 shows how the Derivation Process groups all of these aspects into the four Views at each Modelling Level.

Analogies to the three Modelling Level approach of CIM-OSA can be found in Electronic Circuit Design (Functional, Logical and Physical Design) and in Software Engineering (Requirement Analysis, Logical and Physical Design). However, these are analogies only in terms of a three phase structuring concept. As will be seen later (Chapter 8. CIM-OSA Life Cycle) the content of each of the CIM-OSA Modelling Levels is much richer than any one of these two analogies.

CIM-OSA provides generic building blocks for each Modelling Level starting already with requirement definitions (Requirements Definition Modelling Level). Its Design Specification Modelling Level considers all enterprise constraints (business and system capabilities related) and provides an globally optimised set of enterprise requirements. CIM-OSA also contains in its Implementation Description Modelling Level several levels of system description (Component Specification, Component Selection, Component Implementation, System Qualification and Release).

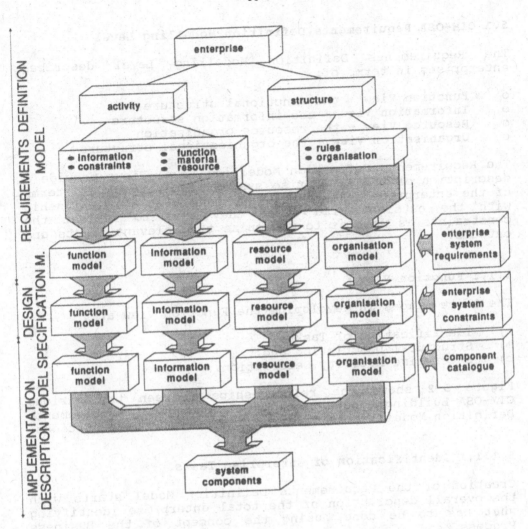

Figure 5-1: CIM-OSA Modelling Levels and Derivation Process for CIM-OSA Particular Architecture

5.1 CIM-OSA Requirements Definition Modelling Level

The Requirements Definition Modelling Level describes enterprises in terms of:

o   **Function View** - the functional structure
o   **Information View** - the information structure
o   **Resource View** - the resource organisation
o   **Organisation View** - the organisational structure

The Requirements Definition Modelling Level Views provide a description of the enterprise system requirements, in terms of the enterprise objectives. They have also a relationship with the outside world since they have to reflect the constraints as well as to recognize the relevant inputs and outputs.

5.1.1 Function View

The three stages in developing the Function View are:

a)   Identification of Tasks,
b)   Structural Description and
c)   Enterprise Activity Description.

Figure 5-2 shows the relationships between the various CIM-OSA Building Blocks used for each stage of Requirements Definition Modelling as described in the following sections.

5.1.1.1 Identification of Enterprise Tasks

Creation of the Requirements Definition Model starts with the overall description of the total enterprise identifying **what** has to be done, using the concept of the Business Process.

Business Process and its Content Definitions:

A **Business Process** is the business user's view of what tasks are required to achieve a particular enterprise objective. A task is a general term which includes Business Processes and Enterprise Activities.

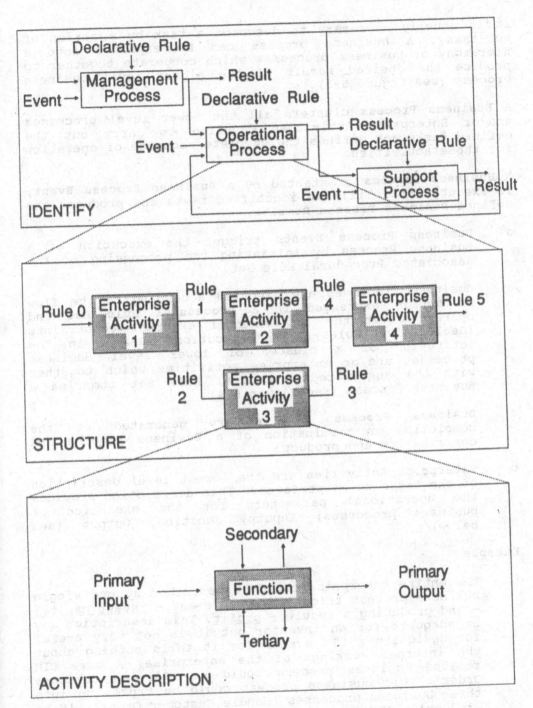

Figure 5-2: Requirements Definition Model Building Blocks

It is usually necessary to describe a task by a series of sub-tasks. A business process can be expanded into a hierarchy of business processes which cooperate together to produce the desired result of the higher level business process (see Figure 5-3).

A **Business Process** clusters all the lower level processes and/or Enterprise Activities required to carry out the defined tasks and defines the complete sequence of operation for these activities.

A **Business Process** is started by a **Business Process Event**, is executed to fulfil the identified tasks and produces the defined **Business Process Results**.

o   **Business Process Events** trigger the execution of a Business Process by initiating the processing of the associated Procedural Rule Set.

o   Business Processes are executed according to the flow of action expressed in a **Procedural Rule Set** and operate under the influence of external constraints (**Declarative Rules**). The execution results in the activation of a cluster of lower level Business processes and/or enterprise activities which together with the associated Procedural Rule Set comprise a Business Process (see Figure 5-4).

o   **Business Process Results** are generated at the completion or termination of a Business Process and describe its end product

o   **Enterprise Activities** are the lowest level description of the tasks to be performed. This description provides the operational parameters for the execution of business processes; Inputs, Function, Output (see below)

Example

The entire enterprise could be described by one single business process triggered by an event - <u>invest capital</u> - and producing a result - <u>profit</u>. This description may be adequate for an investor but it is not very useful for designing a CIM system for it tells nothing about the internal workings of the enterprise. A more CIM related business process could be 'Service Customer Order'. This business process could be broken up into three business processes 'Handle Customer Order', 'Make Product', 'Deliver Product' to describe the tasks necessary to service a customer order. Such a business process would be triggered by the event 'Order' and would produce the result 'Product'.

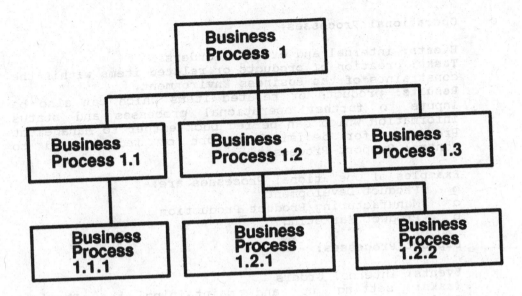

Figure 5-3: Hierarchy of Business Processes

Business Process Categories:

CIM-OSA **categorizes** Business Processes according to their role within the enterprise. Each main category of Business Processes will be further subdivided according to the unique purpose of each Business Process. Three main categories of Business Processes are envisaged (see also Figure 5-2), based upon the role each one plays within the enterprise:-

o **Management Processes:**

Event: relevant changes in the enterprise internal and external environment
Tasks: monitoring/evaluating changes in the internal and external environment and defining corresponding adjustments to the **Business Environment** within which all enterprise tasks are performed.
Results: plans and information used to manage and control other processes.

Examples of Management Processes are:-
o Enterprise Strategy Planning
o Enterprise Operations Planning
o Enterprise Performance Monitoring
o Enterprise Condition Reporting

o   **Operational Processes:**

Events: internal and external orders
Tasks: creation of products or related items within the
constraints of the Business Environment.
Results: products or related items which can also be
inputs to further operational processes and status
information which can be fed back either to Management
Processes for decision support or fed forward to
control Support Processes.

Examples of Operational Processes are:-
o   Product Development
o   Manufacturing/Product Production
o   Product Marketing

o   **Support Processes:**

Events: internal orders
Tasks: setting up and maintaining the **Physical
Environment** required to host the Business Environment.
Results: operational components of the physical
environment and status information on availability
which can be fed back to operational processes and to
management processes.

Examples of Support Processes are:-
o   Plant Installation
o   Plant Maintenance
o   Plant Set-up
o   Plant Repairing

5.1.1.2 Structural Description

The second stage in building the enterprise system from the
business requirements uses the concepts of **Procedural Rule
Sets** and **Enterprise Activities** to provide a structural
description of the enterprise. Each business process is
formally defined by an associated procedural rule set which
describes its behaviour required to achieve the defined
business process result (Figure 5-4).

Business Process Control and Function Definitions:

o   **Procedural Rules Set:** represents the flow of control
between business processes and/or enterprise
activities. They define selection criteria for
executing the cluster lower level Business Processes
and/or enterprise activities.

There is one procedural rule set for each business
process. The rule set contains a series of statements,
one for each enterprise activity or lower level

business process in the cluster, to define what action is required upon completion or termination of each enterprise activity or lower level business process.

o **Enterprise Activities:** define the functionality of the enterprise (Generic Building Blocks).

Enterprise activities are not part of any given business process, but are employed by one or more business processes via their associated procedural rule sets. This relationship allows enterprise activities to be shared between different business processes.

This ensures a separation of functionality Enterprise Activities) and behaviour (Procedural Rule Set) making it possible to revise behaviour, in order to meet changing circumstances, without altering the installed functionality.

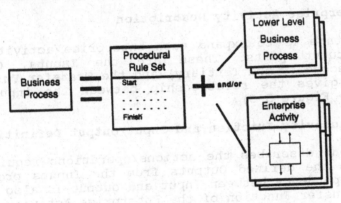

Figure 5-4: Decomposition of Business Process

Enterprise Activity Categories

CIM-OSA categorizes enterprise activities according to their primary purpose (function). Each main category of enterprise activities will be further subdivided according to the unique function of each enterprise activity. Currently we envisage three main categories of enterprise activities each associated with one of the main categories of business processes and each subdivided as shown.:-

o   management oriented enterprise activities:-

Plan
Control
Monitor
Report

o   operational oriented enterprise activities:-

> Develop (Research, Define, Design, Qualify)
> Produce (Rest, Move, Make, Verify)
> Market (Search, Acquire, Sell, Distribute,
>   Maintain)

o   support oriented enterprise activities:-

> Install
> Set-up
> Maintain
> Repair

Additional levels of subdivision may be required to obtain a powerful set of generic building blocks for the functional description of the enterprise.

5.1.1.3 Enterprise Activity Description

The final stage is to expand each enterprise activity into its constituent parts. These are the **Inputs, Outputs** (Primary, Secondary and Tertiary) and the **Transfer Function**. The latter gives the relationship between the inputs and outputs (see Figure 5-5).

Enterprise Activity Function and Input/Output Definitions:

o   **Function:** describes the actions/operations required to produce the defined Outputs from the Inputs provided. This dependency between Input and output is also called the Transfer Function of the Enterprise Activity.

The Enterprise Activity Function is represented at the Design Specification Modelling Level as a set of Functional Operations (see Section 5.2.1).

o   **Input** and **Output:** describes the information (or material) the function needs for its execution and produces as a result of its execution.

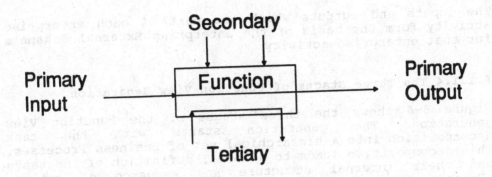

Figure 5-5: Enterprise Activity

The following inputs and outputs exist each with a specific purpose:-

o **Primary:** the objects to be transformed by the function (Input: Data/Material) and the objects resulting from the transformation (Output: Data/Material). The dashed line connecting input with output in Figure 5-5 indicates this transformation.

   We distinguish between **Information** and **Material** as primary input because of their different logistic properties (eg. information can be easily replicated at several sites whilst material cannot).

o **Secondary:** constraints on the transformation by the function (Input) and status of the transformation (Output).

o **Tertiary:** the means (enterprise assets) required to execute the transformation by the function (Input) and status and means returned from the transformation (Output). The dashed line connecting input with output indicates the usage by the function.

Inputs and outputs do not have separate existence apart from the Enterprise Activity Types they are associated with. They are classified according to **Information Classes** as defined within the **Information View**

The inputs and outputs which are part of each enterprise activity form the basis of the enterprise **External Schemata** for that enterprise activity.

5.1.1.4 The Three Stages of Function View Generation

Figure 5-6 shows the three stages of the Function View generation. The generation starts with the task decomposition into a hierarchical set of Business Processes. This decomposition leads to a formal definition of the tasks and their internal structure and sequence of actions (Procedural Rule Sets). This decomposition also leads to the definition of a set of Enterprise Activities. These are the functions, inputs and outputs required to fulfil the requirements defined in the task descriptions.

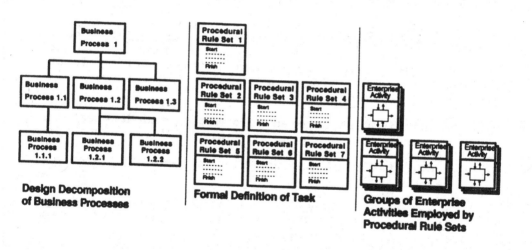

Figure 5-6: Relationship between Stage Results

5.1.2 Information View

To produce a model of a working system which satisfies the business requirements, it is necessary to structure the information inputs and outputs of the enterprise activities into the **Information View** of the **Particular Requirements Definition Model**.

The purpose of the Information View is threefold:

a) to capture the information needs of the particular enterprise, for presentation to the business user and for his verification.

b) to provide sufficient detail to allow Design Specification Views to be derived;

c) to enable the other Views to be generated.

The business user is guided by the **Integrated Enterprise Engineering Environment (IEEE)** in generating the Information View of the Requirements Definition Model. The main inputs to this generation are the information inputs and outputs for the set of enterprise activities beneath a hierarchy of business processes. This generation can either be done for a selection of enterprise activities within a business process, or for all the enterprise activities.

Constructs provided for the Information View are:

o   **Information Class** structures the information according to the user's view

The information inputs and outputs of the enterprise activities will already be allocated to the different Information Classes. This classification will facilitate the dialogue between the business user and the Integrated Enterprise Engineering Environment. This enables the business user to choose from a reduced set of information structures.

o   **Information Item** is the lowest level element in any information class

The business user will be guided during the Instantiation process in formalising the information. Specific details have to be described as attributes to the Information Items.

Business Processes in companies cover areas from management to research and from sales to quality assurance. The AMICE project had to restrict its development work to the manufacturing area. In this scope we deal mainly with product development, manufacturing planning and control, and the production and assembly shop. concentrating on the information handled in these areas, we can define four Information Classes which are of interest to the user:

-   **Product Information**

-   **Manufacturing Planning and Control Information**

-   Shop Floor Information,

-   Basic Information

According to the information structure defined for the Enterprise Activity Inputs and Outputs, CIM-OSA starts Information Classes at that level. Sub-classes may appear in more than one super-class.

Information Classes at Requirements Definition Modelling Level

Information inputs and outputs:

    primary:
        -basic information
        -product information
        -shop floor information
        -planning and control information

    secondary:
        -responsibility information
        -basic information
        -product information
        -shop floor information
        -planning and control information

    tertiary:
        -resources

o   **Product** information describes all features of a product and its production processes. It comprises behavioural, functional and physical aspects of the product such as the Bill of Material, the product geometry, etc. Production process description comprises process plans, CL-data, etc.

o   **Manufacturing Planning and Control** information contains all information necessary for handling orders. Therefore the class contains information like customer or production orders, logistic information concerning raw materials or tool devices, current capacity constraints, etc. The required information are accessed at the shop floor.

o   **Shop Floor** information addresses the current operations in the production and assembly shops. Therefore, we find process oriented information such as shop schedules translated from production orders, the actual use of resources, and technological oriented information such as work procedure descriptions for machine tools.

o   **Basic** information is a platform that supports many
    company departments. It contains the company standards
    and guide-lines, and the equipment and organisation
    descriptions valid for the whole company.

5.1.3 Resource View

During the definition of the business requirements the user
has also defined the required resources as tertiary inputs
of the required enterprise activities. This Information
Class is to be restructured to provide a consistent view of
all the resources needed for a particular part of the
enterprise (one or a set of business processes).

This Resource View is the basis for the Resource Model (see
below) which is required for further organisation of the
resources in terms of physical location, and for identifying
responsibilities.

5.1.4 Organisation View

CIM-OSA considers the definition and identification of
responsibilities a very important subject. Responsibilities
have to be known by the system for exception handling and
human decision making processes. Responsibilities may be
defined for enterprise assets (resources, information,
capital, etc.) or they may be for operational entities
(business processes, products, etc.)

The Organisation View is the basis for the Organisation
Model (see below) which describes all the enterprise
responsibilities.

5.2 CIM-OSA Design Specification Modelling Level

CIM-OSA derives the system description (the Implementation
Description Modelling Level) from the business requirement
definitions (the Requirements Definition Modelling Level).

To isolate the two levels and to reduce the impact of
changes from one level to the other CIM-OSA has defined a
Design Specification Modelling Level which acts as a stable
base between the business requirements definition and the
system description.

In this role the Design Specification Modelling Level
represents the optimised user requirements, taking into
account all the enterprise business and system constraints.
This optimisation is carried out by system organizers which
optimise the different user requirements from a global

enterprise view in terms of business needs and system capabilities (see also Figure 5-1).

The Derivation process itself consists of a set of guide-lines to derive four Design Specification Modelling Level Views from the Requirements Definition Modelling Level Views and another set of guide-lines to derive from them the Implementation Description Modelling Level Views (the system descriptions required for the execution of the CIM system).

The Design Specification Modelling Level consists again of four Views:-

o **Function View** - logical grouping of business processes
o **Information View** - logical grouping of information
o **Resource View** - logical grouping of resources
o **Organisation View** - logical grouping of responsibilities

The most complex aspect is that of information for which CIM-OSA provides a number of unique building blocks for constructing an Information View (see below). Contrary to all other Views which are real models the Information View is a meta model and as such does not contain any real data.

5.2.1 Function View

The Design Specification Function View is logically the realization of the Enterprise Function View. As such it has to link the relevant user requirement definition to the relevant system description at the Implementation Description Modelling Level.

This requires in the Function View of the Design Specification Model a union construct that mediates between the user oriented Function View described in the Requirements Definition Modelling Level and the Implementation oriented Function View of the Implementation Description Model. CIM-OSA therefore defines the so called Implemented Functional Operation (IFO).

This is the smallest unit of work that can be performed by the functional resources (so called Implemented Functional Entities) described in the Function View of the Implementation Description Model. CIM-OSA provides Functional Entity types at the Implementation Level that can perform the following categories of Implemented Functional Operations:

IFO Implemented Functional Operation
    IDO Implemented Data Storage Functional Operation
    IAO Implemented Application Functional Operation
    IHO Implemented Human Functional Operation
    IMO Implemented Machine Functional Operation

Enterprise Activity Types have been defined at the Requirements Definition Modelling Level (Function View) regardless of the availability of real resources. The Enterprise Activity Tertiary Input description specifies the functional category of resources which may contain several options.

Example of tertiary Input:

    "A resource capable to write customer bills"

Now in the Design Specification Modelling under the constraints of available technologies the decision on the style of implementation must be taken.

Example: whether the customer order shall be written by

(1)   a Human Being (Implemented Human Functional Operation
      - IHO)

(2)   automatically by an Application Program (Implemented
      Application Functional Operation - IAO)

However at the Design Specification Level nothing is decided on the real instances of functional components that will be used to implement the IHO respectively the IAO.

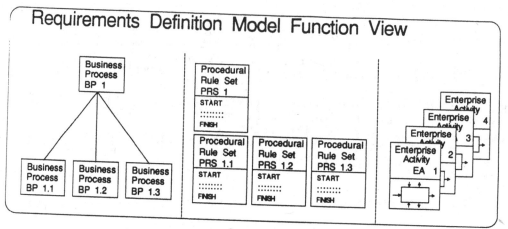

Derivation

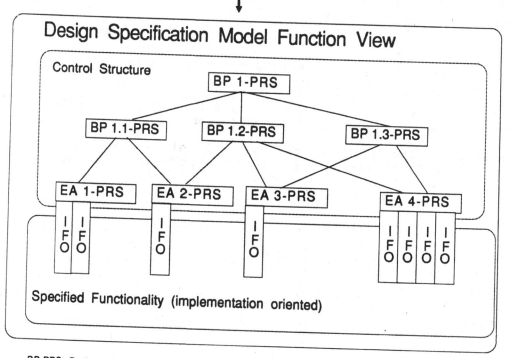

BP-PRS Business Process Procedural Rule Set
EA-PRS Enterprise Activity Procedural Rule Set
IFO   Implemented Functional Operation

Figure 5-7: Derivation of the Design Specification Model Function View.

The Design Specification Model Function View describes the entire Enterprise control structure by a hierarchical structure of interdependent Procedural Rule Sets. The Enterprise Activity internal sequence control is also described by a Procedural Rule Set (Enterprise Activity Procedural Rule Set). These Rule Sets request the execution of the associated set of Implemented Function Operations (see Figure 5-7).

The Implemented Functional Operation is the union element of the Enterprise Function Model and the Implementation Function Model. The Enterprise Function Model specifies by the Enterprise Activities Tertiary Inputs the sets of IFO's required to perform the Enterprise Activities while the Implementation Function Model will provide active Elements (the Implemented Functional Entities - see below) which perform the specified Implemented Functional Operations.

5.2.2 Information View

The **Conceptual Schema** for an enterprise is the major construct used in the Information View at this Modelling Level.

The Particular Requirements Definition Model and the Reference Architecture constructs for the Information View are the main inputs for the creation of the Particular Design Specification Information View (View generation from the Function View is potentially involved). This Creation process (see below) involves executing the Information View - Derivation Process and the Information View - Instantiation Process (and potentially View generation from the Function View). These processes include various CIM-OSA guide-lines, and are combined with the skill and knowledge of the system organisation professional to produce this Information View.

It should be noted that similar procedures exist for the creation of all the other Views at the Design Specification Modelling Level.

5.2.3 Resource View

The Resource View at the Design Specification Modelling Level provides an optimised and balanced set of resources which have to be provided to satisfy the needs of the Enterprise Activities.

o   **Logical Cell** is the CIM-OSA building block for the definition of a group of logically structured resources required to support a set of related enterprise activities.

The primary purpose of Logical Cells is to identify collections of equipment and resources which are candidates for having a high degree of integration because they support groups of functions which require close or frequent interaction. They may be used to reflect a job-oriented structure, or a process-oriented one.

5.2.4 Organisation View

The Organisation View at the Design Specification Modelling Level describe an optimised and balanced organisation of enterprise responsibilities for enterprise assets (resources and information) and for its operational entities (business processes, products, etc.). These responsibilities have to be organized in order to satisfy the needs of the enterprise for decision making.

o **Organisational Cell** is the CIM-OSA building block for grouping responsibilities within an enterprise.

The Organisational Cell provide a basis from which decisions on the timely provision of resources and data needed for the execution of Enterprise Activities can be enabled and from which decisions can be made on the enterprise operation.

Relationship between Resource and Organisation View

Figure 5-8 illustrates how the two Views provide their contribution to the structuring of resources. The logical structure of the resources (Logical Cells - LC) consider the equipment according to its use by Enterprise Activities. Logical Cells collect all resource objects (human beings, machines, data storage capabilities, data processing capabilities, etc.) required for implementation of one or a group of Enterprise Activities.

On the other hand Organisational Cells (OC) structure the enterprise resources according to their provision or their identified responsibilities. Both Views provide relevant information for the arrangement of resources by the **Resource Management** Service (see below) of the Integrating Infrastructure (IIS).

Such relationships exist also for other identified responsibilities in the Organisation View and their related Enterprise Objects in the other Views (Information and Function View).

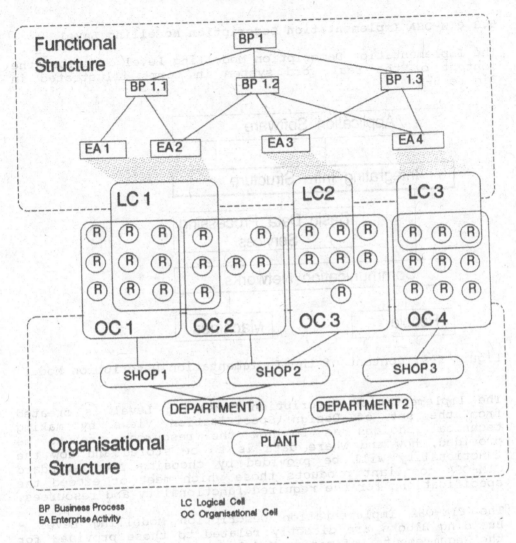

Figure 5-8: Relationship between Resource View and
Organisation View

5.3 CIM-OSA Implementation Description Modelling Level

The Implementation Description Modelling Level describes the content of the real word system in terms illustrated in Figure 5-9.

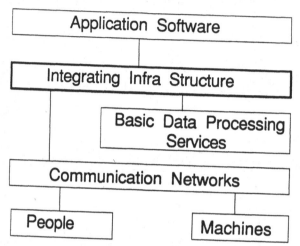

Figure 5-9: Content of the Implementation Description Model

The Implementation Description Modelling Level is created from the set of Design Specification Views by making technical choices as to how the resources are to be provided, how and where data is to be stored and how the functionality will be provided by choosing from standard CIM-OSA compliant products those which meet or exceed the specifications for the required functionality and resources.

The CIM-OSA Implementation Description Modelling Level - Building Blocks are directly related to those provided for the Requirements Definition Model. Thus there will be a fair chance that system components required will already exist in the market place, or can easily be implemented from an existing CIM-OSA specification.

Like all other Modelling Levels, the Implementation Description Modelling Level comprises the four Views:

o   **Function View -**   operational structure of Enterprise
                  Activity Functions
o   **Information View -** operational structure of enterprise
                  information
o   **Resource View -**   operational structure of enterprise
                  resources (incl. specifications of
                  Implemented Components)
o   **Organisation View -** operational structure of enterprise
                  organisational

The Implementation Description Model (Figure 5-10) is thus a description of the real world processes of the enterprise, in terms of all the tangible components used in its CIM system. These components are divided into two groups:

1) **Manufacturing Technology** required to process materials, assemble products, pack and move them. Manufacturing Technology includes both people and their associated workplans and machines with their required control programs.

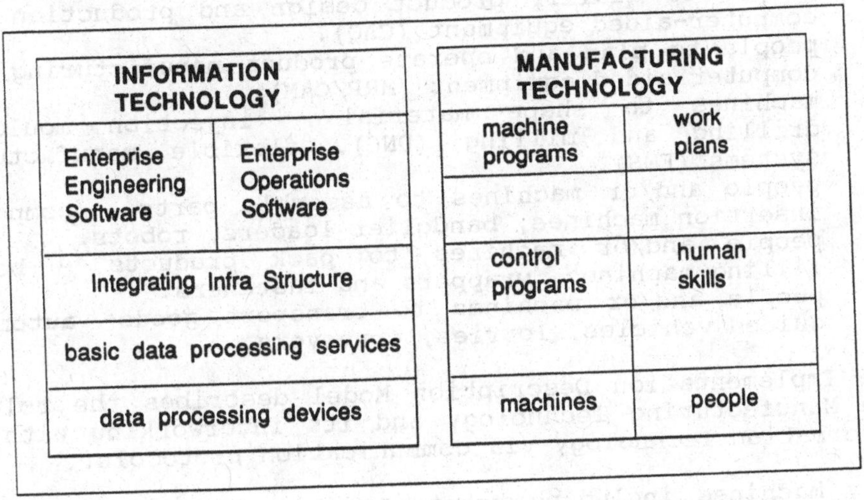

INFORMATION TECHNOLOGY		MANUFACTURING TECHNOLOGY	
Enterprise Engineering Software	Enterprise Operations Software	machine programs	work plans
Integrating Infra Structure		control programs	human skills
basic data processing services			
data processing devices		machines	people

Figure 5-10: Components described in the Implementation Description Model

2) **Information Technology** required to process and distribute data for all activities in the enterprise. The Information Technology therefore includes the application programs, plus the CIM-OSA **Integrating Infrastructure**. The latter consists of all the **CIM-OSA Services** that support the execution of application software by allowing them to run on the host hardware, while keeping application programs and hardware independent of each other. These CIM-OSA services also support the Manufacturing Technology components by enabling them to communicate with the host system and each other.

In addition to these operational concerns provision must also be made for the maintenance and revision of the enterprise environment for each operational task. Thus the CIM-OSA Integrated Enterprise Engineering Environment must also be a component of the installed Information Technology.

5.3.1 System Description: Manufacturing Technology Components

Manufacturing Components embrace the widest possible aspects of manufacturing technology :-

o   people to manage and operate computer supported enterprise systems or parts thereof (CIM).
o   people to design and develop products with computer-aided equipment (CAD).
o   people to qualify product design and production with computer-aided equipment (CAQ).
o   people to plan and operate product manufacturing with computer aided equipment (MRP/CAM).
o   machines to shape material - injection moulding, drilling and milling (DNC), flexible manufacturing systems (FMS).
o   people and/or machines to assemble parts - component insertion machines, bandolier loaders, robots.
o   people and/or machines to pack products - bottle filling machines, wrappers and fasteners.
o   people and/or machines to transport goods- automatic guided vehicles, lorries, conveyers.

The Implementation Description Model describes the role of the Manufacturing Technology and its interworking with the Information Technology via communication protocols.

Many machines including robots, machine tools, FMS contain 'intelligence' i.e. computer-like features. However, they are considered to be part of Manufacturing Technology since this intelligence is physically imbedded within the physical components.

People who performe physical work are referred to within the Implementation Description Model as part of Manufacturing Technology. Since they are an essential component of a CIM system it is necessary to describe them in functional terms.

5.3.2 System Description: Information Technology Components

Information Technology components are categorized under two headings - Basic Data Processing Resources and Application Software.

Basic data processing resources include:-
o   Integrating Infrastructure
o   computer hardware
o   communications networks
o   basic software including microcode and firmware
o   operating system software to control computer resources
o   database management systems
o   language compilers

o   'housekeeping' and other supervisory software

Application software is written for a particular application and issued as a CIM-OSA compliant software package.

All the items referred to as basic data processing resources are within the Integrated Data Processing Environment part of the Implementation Description Model.

5.3.3 Function View

The Function View of the Implementation Description Modelling Level is created from the Function View of the Requirements Definition Modelling Level (via the Design Specification Modelling Level). The Enterprise Function View is designed as a executable flat (network) control and functional structure containing:

o   a hierarchical structure of Business Processes (BP) representing the control structure in form of one Procedural Rule Set (BP-PRS) for every Business Process,

o   a non hierarchical pool of Enterprise Activities (EA) that can be executed on request of the superimposed Level of Business Processes.

o   a Transfer Function of Enterprise Activities which can be regarded as an active element with an internal decomposition into operational units, the **Implemented Functional Operations** and their own control structure, the Enterprise Activity Procedural Rule Set (EA-PRS).

Section 5.2 above introduced the internal decomposition of the Enterprise Activity and its control structure. The constructs defined are part of the Design Specification Modelling Level (refer back to Figure 5-7).

o   **Implemented Functional Operation** (IFO) is the smallest controllable unit of work implemented by real data processing objects. In other words, the Implemented Enterprise Activity does not perform any work, but specifies the work to be done by its set of Implemented Functional Operations.

o   **Enterprise Activity Procedural Rule Set is modelled on the Business Process Procedural Rule Set. It controls the execution of Implemented Functional Operations associated with the Enterprise Activity.**

In a real enterprise the total control structure will consist of thousands of Instances of Business Process Control Elements (Procedural Rule Sets) normally organized in a multi level hierarchy. The pool of Enterprise Activity occurrences may also amount to thousands.

This complex structure developed and maintained during the Requirements Definition Model design and restructured in the Design Specification Model design has now to be mapped onto a distributed processing environment consisting of both computers and people. All of its components are linked by multiple communication systems. In order to tackle the mapping problem, the complex control and functional structure must be reorganized into a structure of distributable processing entities.

Distributable processing entities must be designed according to the following guide-line:

> each entity represents an area of responsibility cooperating with partner entities in a loosely coupled mode.

CIM-OSA therefore defines the basic construct for the functional description of distributed functionality:

o the **Functional Entity (FE)** which is an abstract object capable of processing and storing information. For information exchange any two cooperating Functional Entities use the mechanism of Transaction.

o **Transaction** is based on the principle of Request-Action-Response.

A detailed description of the Functional Entity construct is given in Section 7.3.

The entire processing system of an Enterprise is described in the implemented Function View as a nested hierarchy of Functional Entities (Fig. 5-11).

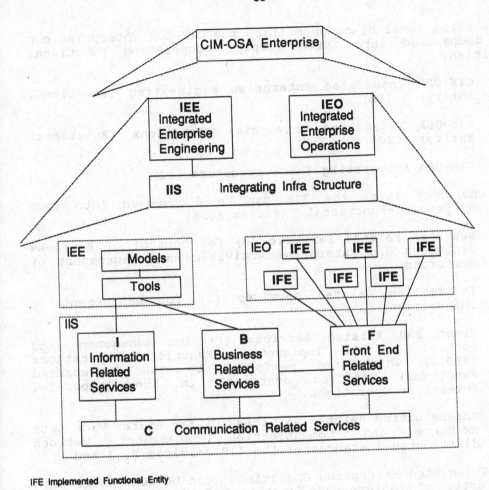

IFE Implemented Functional Entity

Figure 5-11: Implementation Level Functional Decomposition
of the CIM-OSA Enterprise

In a first level of decomposition the CIM-OSA Enterprise can be decomposed into three complex cooperating Functional Entities:

o   **CIM-OSA Integrated Enterprise Engineering** (Functional Entity) (IEE)

o   **CIM-OSA Integrated Enterprise Operations (Functional Entity) (IEO)**

o   **CIM-OSA Integrating Infra Structure** (IIS)

At the next level the IIS can be decomposed into four primary Service-Functional Entities (SFE)

o   **Business Related Services** (B) for control of Business Processes and Enterprise Activities and management of Resources.

o   **Information Related Services** (I) for management of Information.

o   **Front End Related Services** (F) for management and control of the Implemented Functional Operations (IFO's) which are performed by the Implemented Functional Entities contained in the Integrated Enterprise Operations.

o   **Communication Related Services** (C) for System Wide Data exchange and Communication Management between distributed instances of the IIS services B, I and F.

The Integrated Enterprise Operations can be decomposed into a cluster of **Implemented Functional Entities** (IFE). These are categorized according to the Implemented Functional Operations

```
IFE  Implemented Functional Entity
       IDF Implemented Data Storage Functional Entity
       IAF Implemented Application Functional Entity
       IHF Implemented Human Functional Entity
       IMF Implemented Machine Functional Entity
```

Figure 5-12 illustrates how the Enterprise Function View shown in Figure 5-7 is mapped onto the Implemented Function View.

The example assumes that the Enterprise Control Structure (Business Process and Enterprise Activity Procedural Rule Sets) shall be distributed over two CIM-OSA-nodes. Each node consists of an Instance of the IIS-Functional Entity Types

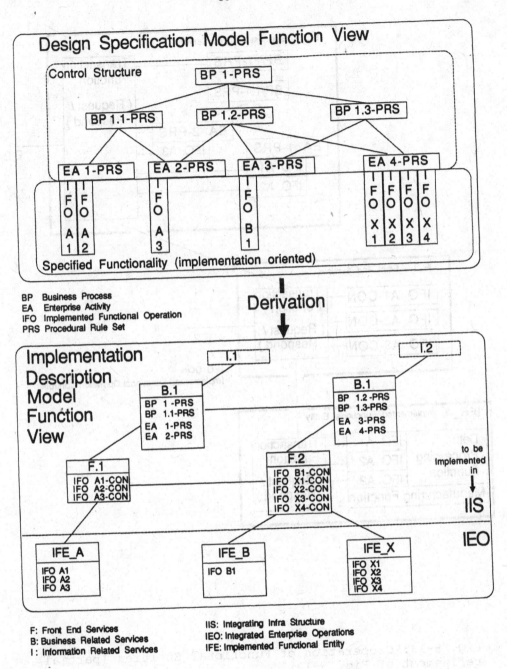

Fig. 5-12: Mapping the Design Specification Function View onto the Implementation Description Functional View

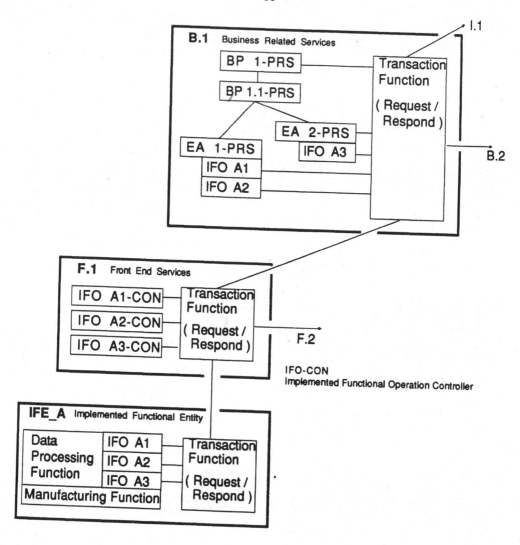

Fig. 5-13: Cooperation of Functional Entities (partial refinement of Fig. 5-12)

o   **Business Related Services** (B)
o   **Front End Related Services** (F)
o   **Information Related Services** (I)

The Procedural Rule Sets are distributed over the two peer entities of Business Related-Services as indicated in Figure 5-12.

The Implemented Functional Operations (IFO) are assumed to be performed by three Implemented Functional Entities A, B and X. They are controlled by the IFO-Controllers (IFO-CON) contained in the Front End Services (F) of the IIS as indicated in the Figure 5-12.

Figure 5-13 expands the Business Related Services shown in Figure 5-12. This Figure explains the principle of transaction oriented cooperation of the distributed portions of the Enterprise Functions. Essential are the Request-Respond Blocks which provide the transaction oriented communication mechanism for the end-to-end synchronization of the overall control structure.

5.3.4 Information View

Similar to the Function View mapping, the Enterprise Informations Relationship Structure is mapped onto Instances of the IIS Service Functional Entity

o   **Information Related Services** (I)

and the Information Objects are grouped into

o   **Implemented Data Storage Functional Entities** (IDF)

This is illustrated in Figure 5-14.

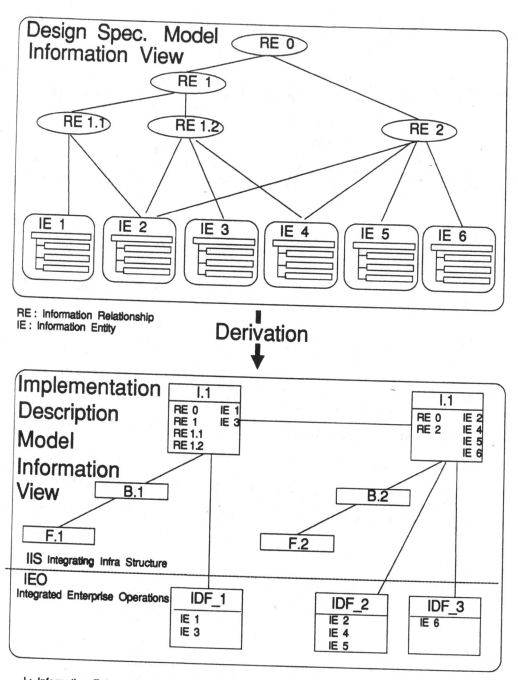

Fig. 5-14: Derivation of the Implementation Description
Model Information View

5.3.5 Resource View

The Function View described in Section 5.3.3 consists of a structure of communicating Functional Entities performing functions and controls described in the Enterprise Function View. The Functional Entity construct abstractly describes a behaviour and not a real physical equipment. However the categorisation into one of the Implemented Functional Entity (IFE) Types

o   Implemented Human Functional Entity (IHF)
o   Implemented Application Functional Entity (IAF)
o   Implemented Machine Functional Entity (IMF)
o   Implemented Data Storage Functional Entity (IDF)

indicates the means of realization. The set of Implemented Functional Operations (IFO) associated with each Implemented Functional Entity specifies its Type further (e.g. whether it is to drill, cut, mould etc.)

Implemented Functional Entities have to be supported by a set of implemented components called

o   Implemented (Functional Entity) Component Set (ICS)

The Resource View shows all the Implemented Functional Entities identified in the Function View in connection with their supporting Implemented Component Sets. This is illustrated in Figure 5-15.

This View is derived from the Logical Cells defined in the Design Specification Level Resource View (see Section 5.2.3 and Figure 5-8). The difference between the two Views is that Implemented Component Sets describe the real physical equipment on which the Functional Entities are implemented. The Logical Cells describe the grouping of logical resources without declaring definite instances of hardware.

5.3.6 Organisation View

This View follows from the Design Specification Level Organisation View described in Section 5.2.4 (Figure 5-8). The latter describes the organisation of enterprise responsibilities (like departments, divisions, shops etc.) The Implemented Organisation View shows beside other responsibilities (for Information, Business Processes, etc.) the responsibilities for configurations of the real physical equipment that realizes the Enterprise Operation. The construct used here is the

Organisational Component Set (OCS)

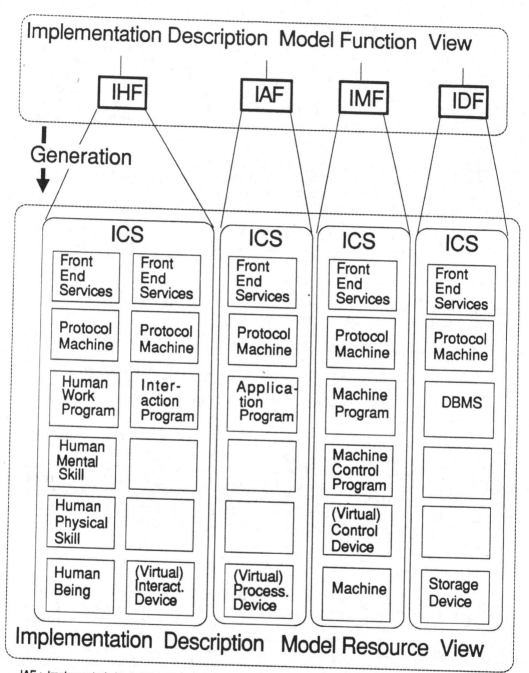

Figure 5-15: Implementation Description Model Resource View

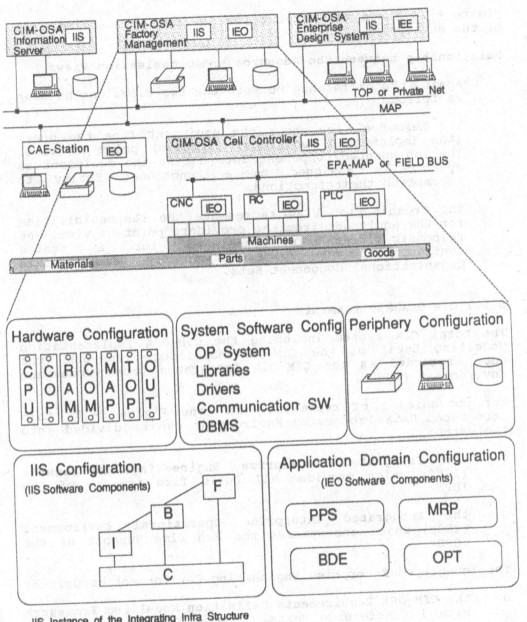

Figure 5-16: Elements of the Implemented Organisation Model

Figure 5-16 shows this aspect for the data processing area of the enterprise.

Relationship between the Resource and Organisation Views

Again, the difference between the two Views can be seen as follows.

The Resource View shows the equipment from the users (the Implemented Functional Entities) point of view. The Implemented Component Sets define the equipment as dynamically assigned to a Functional Entity to accomplish their functions.

The Organisation View represents the responsibilities for the equipment from the providers point of view. The responsibilities are assigned for a static configuration of devices physically grouped into Organisational Component Sets.

5.3.7 CIM-OSA Environments

The total CIM system including the CIM-OSA Implementation Modelling Level of the CIM-OSA Modelling Framework (the Cube) regarded as the CIM-OSA Integrated Data Processing Environment (IDPE).

For convenience of representation (see Figure 5-17) this Integrated Data Processing Environment can be divided into two parts:

o   the **Integrated Enterprise Engineering Environment** (IEEE) which provides all Build Time aspects of the IDPE

o   the **Integrated Enterprise Operational Environment** (IEOE) which encompasses the Run Time Support of the IDPE

The Integrated Enterprise Engineering Environment comprises:

o   the **CIM-OSA Requirements Definition Modelling Framework** with its Reference Parts (Generic Constructs, Partial Models) and the resulting Particular Models (design version) of the particular enterprise.

o   the **CIM-OSA Integrated Enterprise Engineering Functions** (IEE) which is a set of CAE tools to support the Requirements Definition Model Creation Process.

o   the relevant services of the **CIM-OSA Integrating Infrastructure** (IIS) supporting the IEE.

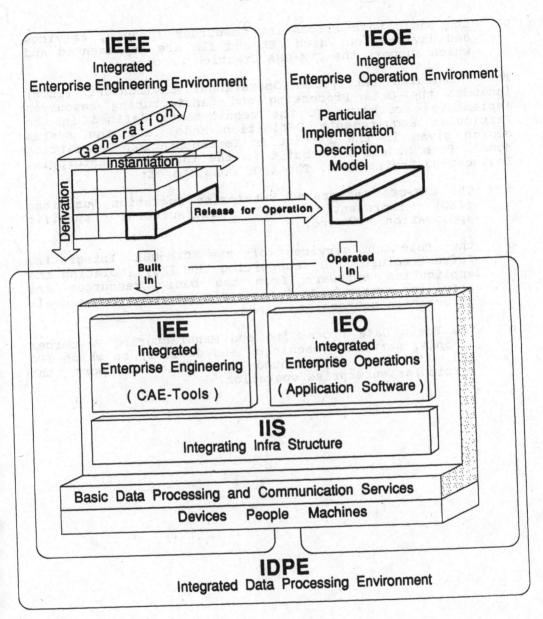

Fig. 5-17: Overview of CIM-OSA Environments

o   the Basic Data Processing Resources (people, services and devices) on which IEE and IIS are implemented and which support the CIM-OSA Creation Process.

The Integrated Enterprise Operational Environment (IEOE) includes the Data Processing and Manufacturing resources implemented according to the requirements defined in the Particular Requirements Definition Model and the system design given in the Particular Implementation Description Model. Both Models were built in the Integrated Enterprise Engineering Environment. The IEOE consists of:

o   The **CIM-OSA Integrated Enterprise Operation Functions** (IEO) representing all manufacturing specific application software.

o   the relevant services of the **CIM-OSA Integrating Infrastructure** (IIS) supporting the IEO, isolating the application software from the basic resources and providing system wide information exchange between all information sources and sinks.

o   the Basic Data Processing and Manufacturing Resources (people, services, machines and devices) on which IEO and IIS are implemented and which support the particular enterprise operation.

6. The Parts of the CIM-OSA Framework and their Relations

This Chapter concentrates on the positioning of the CIM-OSA architectural constructs and their relations with each other. Starting from the Requirements Definition Modelling Level the different constructs used in the Creation Process of the Particular Models are identified.

A detailed positioning of the currently identified CIM-OSA constructs is given in Section 6.3.

6.1 CIM-OSA Architectural Levels

The 2 Reference Architecture Levels of CIM-OSA contain all the constructs required to model the business requirements of a particular enterprise.

The Reference Architecture Levels contain basic constructs at the **Generic Building Block** Level and Macro Constructs at the **Partial Model** Level. The macro constructs are Partial Models since they represent in generic form larger areas (Purchasing) or specific aspects (MRP) of a manufacturing enterprise. These macro constructs are created from relevant basic constructs. For the creation of the **Particular Architecture** instances of both types of constructs are used.

The relations between the different Architectural Levels are expressed in the instantiation process and in the relevant user guide-lines.

The internal structure (Modelling Levels and Views) and the different constructs of the CIM-OSA Architectural Levels are described in the following:

6.2 CIM-OSA Modelling and View Levels

The three Modelling Levels allow modelling of the user aspects and the CIM system aspects of the enterprise. The relations between the different levels are expressed in the relevant derivation processes and user guidelines.

The **Requirements Definition Modelling Level** provides all the means to gather the business requirements of a particular enterprise. Different aspects (Views - see below) can be isolated from the requirements and can be optimised (e.g. by simulation) according to user defined criteria.

The **Design Specification Modelling Level** provides all the means for an optimised and logically restructured representation of the requirements gathered in the Requirements Definition Model. This is a non-redundant and system oriented description of the business requirements.

The **Implementation Description Modelling Level** provides all the means to translate the Design Specification Modelling Level content into a complete system description of all specified, selected and implemented components of the CIM system. From CIM vendor catalogues relevant components are selected and implemented in the enterprise CIM system. These component descriptions together with other relevant information (flow of action, responsibilities) is the content of the Implementation Description Modelling Level.

The 4 different Views (Function, Information, Resource, Organisation) on each Modelling Level allow to Model and to optimise specific user aspects and specific CIM system aspects of the enterprise.

The relations between different Views on the same Modelling Level are expressed by the generation process. The relations between the same View on different Modelling Levels are described by the derivation process. Guide-lines will be provided for user instructions.

In the following the constructs of each of the 4 Views on the different Modelling Levels are described:

6.3 CIM-OSA View Level Constructs and Their Relations

Figure 6-1 summarizes the present definition of CIM-OSA constructs and their distribution across the different Modelling Levels and Views. All the constructs are mapped onto the Generic Level of the CIM-OSA Reference Architecture. The distribution represents the current thinking in the project. It is by no means finite.

The following sections provide a more detailed description of the constructs, their content and their relations with other constructs. These relations may occur across or between Modelling Levels.

6.3.1 Function View

Constructs at the Requirements Definition Modelling Level:

o **Business Processes** consisting of: Business Process Events, Tasks, Procedural Rule Sets and Business Process Results.

   Business processes allow to describe the flow of action in the enterprise.

o **Enterprise Activities** consisting of: Inputs, Function, Outputs

Enterprise activities allow the description of the enterprise actions and their required inputs and outputs.

o   Relation between constructs: via the Procedural Rule Set and the Business Process Events.

Relation established at Particular Architecture Level.

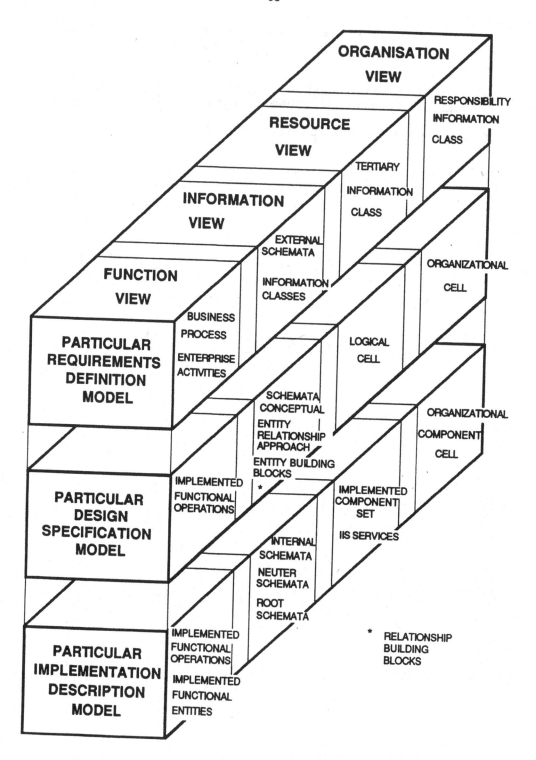

Fig. 6-1: Overview of CIM-OSA Constructs

Constructs at the Design Specification Modelling Level:

o Non-redundant representation of all business processes and enterprise activities derived from the Enterprise Function View .

o **Implemented Functional Operations** represent the breakdown of the functional content of enterprise activities.

Implemented Functional Operations provide the bridge between the Requirements Definition Modelling Level and the Implementation Description Modelling Level.

Constructs at the Implementation Description Modelling Level:

o **Implemented Functional Operations** represent the breakdown of the functional content of enterprise activities.

Implemented Functional operations are the functional description of the specified, selected and implemented components enterprise CIM system (static and dynamic). This includes all Information Technology and Manufacturing Technology components.

o **Implemented Functional Entities** are objects which carry out the functional operations at execution time.

Functional Entities relate to the resource structure derived from the Design Specification Resource View.

Relation between Constructs at all Modelling Levels:

o Relation between Requirements Definition Modelling Level and Implementation Description Modelling Level: via the explicit functional content breakdown of the enterprise activity.

Relation established at Reference Architecture Levels.

6.3.2 Information View

Constructs at the Requirements Definition Modelling Level:

o **External Schemata** representing the Inputs and Outputs of Enterprise Activities.

o **Information Classes** represented as part of the external schemata which structure the Inputs and Outputs of the enterprise activities

Information Classes identified are:

Primary, Secondary Tertiary each one may consist of several levels of subclasses like

- administrative/production information like: cost occurred, time used or planned, order numbers, customer or employee identifications, operating plans, production schedules, organisational responsibilities, etc.

- technical/product information like: material specifications, product specifications, product descriptions (geometry), test data, bill of material, process plans, etc.
- resource information like: capacity available, resource descriptions, etc.
- Organisation information like responsibilities in the different CIM system life cycle phases for: business processes, enterprise activities, resources, information, organisation, etc.

o Relation between constructs: via external schematas.

Relation established at Reference Architecture Level.

Constructs at the Design Specification Modelling Level:

o **Conceptual Schemata** derived from the Requirements Definition Modelling Level Information View in a restructured form and with all redundancies removed.

o **Entity Relationship Approach** to represent the different schemata.

o **Entity Building Blocks** consisting of a group of Enterprise Objects, Enterprise Object Views, and Information Elements.

o **Relationship Building Blocks** consisting of Relations Group to Group, Group to Enterprise Object and Object to Group, Enterprise Object to Enterprise Object, View to View

o Relation between constructs: via conceptual schema and entity relationship approach.

Constructs at the Implementation Description Modelling Level:

o **Internal Schemata, Neuter Schemata** and **Root Schemata** derived from the conceptual schema of the Design Specification Information Model and from instantiated internal schemata building blocks or the Partial Model.

Relation between Constructs at all Modelling Levels:

o   Relations between the different Modelling Level constructs is via the conceptual schema.

     Relation established at reference and Particular Architecture Level.

6.3.3 Resource View

Constructs at the Requirements Definition Modelling Level:

o   consists of the resource information class structured according to user specific evaluation criteria (clustering of resources for: capacity optimization's, flexibility or efficiency of use, physical location, etc.)

Constructs at the Design Specification Modelling Level:

o   **Logical Cell:** logically restructures the resources defined by the enterprise activity tertiary inputs and outputs according to system relevant constraints.

     It is the restructured non-redundant representation of the resource information class relating them to business processes or other structuring criteria.

Constructs at the Implementation Description Modelling Level:

o   **Implemented Component Set** represent the physical resources implemented in the enterprise.

     Implemented Components are related to the Implemented Functional Entities and act as the operational units of resources.

     These include the implemented IIS Services.

Relation between Constructs at all Modelling Levels:

o   Relations between the different Modelling Level constructs is via logical cells.

     Relation established at Particular Architecture Level.

6.3.4 Organisation View

Constructs at the Requirements Definition Modelling Level:

o consists of the organisation information class structured according to user specific evaluation criteria (clustering of responsibilities for: information management (user authorization, access control, etc.), flexibility and optimization's of decision making, optimization's of span of control, visibility of conflicts of interest, etc.)

Constructs at the Design Specification Modelling Level:

o **Organisational Cell:** logically restructures the responsibilities defined by the business process and enterprise activity responsibility definitions according to enterprise relevant constraints.

The Organisational Cell is the restructured, non-redundant, representation of the responsibility information relating to business processes or other structuring criteria.

Constructs at the Implementation Description Modelling Level:

o contains the organisation structure of the enterprise derived from the Design Specification Organisation Model and from instantiated organisation building blocks or Partial Models. It represents the responsibilities in the enterprise for all enterprise operations.

o **Organisational Component Set** are constructs which structure the responsibilities for resources specifically.

Relation between Constructs at all Modelling Levels:

o Relations between the different Modelling Level constructs is via organisational cells.

Relation established at Particular Architecture Level.

Relations between constructs across different Views at the same Modelling Level:

o Requirements Definition Modelling Level: via the information classes.

o Design Specification Modelling Level: via the conceptional schema and the entity relationship approach.

o Implementation Description Modelling Level: yet to be defined.

7. Detailed Description of CIM-OSA

The AMICE project work first concentrated on those specific areas of CIM-OSA which were considered to be the key elements of the architecture:

o   Requirements Definition Modelling Level - Function and Information View
o   Design Specification Modelling Level - Information View
o   Implementation Description Modelling Level - Function and Resource View for specific Information Technology components only (Integrated Infrastructure - IIS)

The following sections present the resulting functional specifications for the CIM-OSA AD0.5 architectural constructs defined.

7.1 CIM-OSA Requirements Definition Modelling Level Constructs

The generic CIM-OSA architectural constructs ('building blocks') defined in the Requirements Definition Modelling Level are shown in the following, using textual 'description templates'. The template for each generic construct defines the constituent parts of the construct, and provides a brief description of how each of those parts is to be defined.

Where CIM-OSA identifies and defines several **types** of a given building block (e.g., Management, Operational and Support Business Process types), one partially-completed template is defined for each type. Such templates fix certain fields of the description template of the underlying building block from which the type has been derived.

7.1.1 Business Process Event

Type: [relevant category - select from list]

Identifier: [relation to other events]

Name: [name of event]

GENERATED BY: [name of event source]

TRIGGERS: [name of procedural rule set (= name of business process]

7.1.2 Business Process

Type: [relevant category - select from list]

Identifier: [relation to other business processes]

Name: [name of business process]

Responsible: [name of responsible entity (person, etc.)]

Comprises: [list of business processes or enterprise activities used]

FUNCTION: [short textual description of the task performed by the business process]

EVENT: [name of enterprise event that triggers the activation of the business process]

RESULT: [name of business result that the business process creates]

PROCEDURAL RULE: [name of procedural rule set (same name as business process]

DECLARATIVE RULE: [name of declarative rule]

7.1.3 Business Process Result

Type: [relevant category - select from list]

Identifier: [relation to other business result]
                        [relation to related business process]

Name: [name of business process result]

Responsible: [name of responsible entity (person, etc.)]

GENERATED BY: [name of business process]

RESULT: [textual description of what is created by the business process]

USED BY: [name of at least one expected user of result (ie business process/external customer)]

7.1.4 Procedural Rule Set

Type:	[relevant category - select from list]
Identifier:	[relation to other procedural rule set] [relation to related business process]
Name:	[name of procedural rule set = name of business process]
PROCESS LOGIC:	[description in the form: "Wait for Enterprise Activity 'X' to end with status 'Y' and then trigger Enterprise Activity 'Z'"]

Wait For	Ending Status	Trigger
PR1. START	[value]	[EA name]
PR2. [EA name]	[value]	[EA name]
	[value]	[EA name], [EA Name]
	Default	Terminate&Inform
PR3. [EA name]	[value]	[EA name]
	[value]	[EA name], [EA Name]
	Default	Terminate&Inform
PR4A [EA name]	[value]	
[EA name]	[value]	[EA name]
	Default	Terminate&Inform
PR4B [EA name]	[value]	
[EA name]	[value]	[EA name]
	Default	Terminate&Inform
PR5. [EA name]	-------	FINISH

A first set of Procedural Rule Types has been identified

PROCEDURAL RULE TYPE: **Forced - FO**

Wait For	Ending Status	Trigger
[EA name]	Default	[EA name]

PROCEDURAL RULE TYPE: **Go/NoGo - GN**

Wait For	Ending Status	Trigger
[EA name]	[value]	[EA name]
	Default	Terminate&Inform

PROCEDURAL RULE TYPE: **Conditional** - CO

Wait For	Ending Status	Trigger
[EA name]	[value1]	[EA name]
	[value2]	[EA name]
	[value3]	[EA name]
	Default	Terminate&Inform

PROCEDURAL RULE TYPE: **Spawning** - SP

Wait For	Ending Status	Trigger
[EA name]	[value1]	[EA name]
		[EA name]
		[EA name]
		[EA name]
	[value2]	[EA name]
		[EA name]
	Default	Terminate&Inform

PROCEDURAL RULE TYPE: **Rendezvous** - RE

	Wait For	Ending Status	Trigger
A	[EA name]	[value1]	
	[EA name]		
	[EA name]		
			[EA name]
B	[EA name]	[value2]	
	[EA name]		
			[EA name]
			[EA name]
		Default	Terminate&Inform

7.1.5 Declarative Rule

Type:	[relevant category - select from list]
Identifier:	[relation to other declarative rules]
Name:	[name of declarative rule]
USED BY:	[name of business process(es)/enterprise activity(ies)]
CONSTRAINTS:	[list of constraints]
CONDITIONS:	[list of conditions for applying rule]

7.1.6 Enterprise Activity

Type: [relevant category - select from list]

Identifier: [relation to other enterprise activity]

Name: [name of enterprise activity]

Responsible: [name of responsible entity (person, etc.)]

INPUTS

- Primary: [object to be transformed]

- Secondary: [constraints on the transformation process definitions, work instructions, product information, production information, task completion criteria, etc]

- Tertiary: [means required to execute the transformation (people with specific skills or experience, plant/machines, capital, equipment, tools, etc.]

FUNCTION: [semi formal description of the transformation <VERB><NOUN><QUALIFIER><TIME><PRIORITY>]

OUTPUTS

- Primary: [the transformed object]

- Secondary: [the resultant status of the transformation itself]

- Tertiary: [the unused part of the resources and the resultant status those resources]

7.2 CIM-OSA Information Model

The Information Model for a particular enterprise covers the transition from the Enterprise Information View to the Implementation Information View.

The description of the data collected, produced and used by a particular enterprise is accomplished using the ISO recommended three schema approach (refer to the ISO TC97/SC5/WG3 and ANSI SPARC Data Base Management System Study Group Report, 1976).

Schemata are building blocks for describing information. These cover the central rationalized description of all enterprise information (the conceptual schema), the description of the physical storage structure for the information (the internal schema) and the way information must be presented outside the storage system (the external schema). The main advantage of this approach is to isolate the requirements from the solution and so to minimise the disruptive influence of one another. It has to serve as a focal point in an environment in which the same information is shared by more than one user, each having his own view of the data representing this shared information. It is also a stable point of reference when an element of an internal or external schema has to be modified.

All the CIM-OSA conceptual schemata are drawn following the Entity Attribute Relationship approach.

It makes use of :

1. **Entities** : which are any concrete or abstract things in the universe of discourse for instance: purchase order 75, the employee John Smith...

2. **Relationships**: which are association between entities. For instance if "John Smith" and "Amsterdam" are two entities, then the fact that "John Smith" lives in "Amsterdam" is considered to be a relationship.

3. **Attributes**: which are the representation of a property of an entity or of a relationship. For instance: the date of the purchase order, the age of John Smith.

The external schemata (representing the external information requirements of the enterprise) have been created by the Integrated Enterprise Engineering Environment (IEEE) while generating the Enterprise Information View.

The internal schema is concerned with the storage of and access to the information at model Run Time. Additional Schemata (Neuter and Root Schema) are defined at the Implementation Description Modelling Level.

The Particular Requirements Definition Information View is represented by a collection of external schemata. Hence it may contain duplicated information, as well as the same information seen from different standpoints.

An external schema identifies how the information described by the conceptual schema is perceived outside the storage system, by a particular user or a particular application, the term User View is sometimes used.

7.2.1 Information View - Instantiation Process

The Information View - Instantiation Process involves guidance from the IEEE on selecting the appropriate Partial Information View and adding information building blocks from the catalogue to arrive at the required view.

In the instantiation process, some generic building blocks will be purely copied to the Particular Level, while others will need to be refined, extended or actualized by parameter values, by making a wide use of information element types, which can be predefined at the Generic Level. Throughout the Information View build-up, information element types must thus easily be accessible and applied.

7.2.2 Information View - Derivation Process

The Information View - Derivation Process includes the following:

- Resolve any conflicts and remove redundancy from the Information View of the Particular Requirements Definition Model.

- Fully identify all the entities and the relationships between them (EAR approach).

- Define all the attributes of each entity and each relationship.

- Structure the technical information according to the information management concepts defined in CIM-OSA (concepts of Enterprise Object, View etc..).

At this Level, the classes of information defined at the Requirements Definition Modelling Level (planning and control, basic, product and shop floor) will be further subdivided in:

- technical information.

- administrative information.

The purpose of this classification is to solve typical problems of information management in CIM.

Example:

Every employees of the company may be depicted by an occurrence of the Entity : employee

The entity type "employee" has the following attribute:

- employee-name
- employee-function
- entry-date

Attributes may take a value on a domain described by simple data types (e.g. numeric value, character string).

Such a model is, of course only a very elementary description of the employee, but we suppose here that these would be the only characteristics that the enterprise wants to deal with. Therefore the adjective "simple" does not apply to the object itself but to the sophistication of the model required by the enterprise.

The enterprise has to manage much more complex information structures, for instance, the automobile currently in design. This management requires a more elaborate model.

- Complex enterprise objects are generally described by a set of submodels, each addressing one aspect of the object; we call them Views.

- Each of these views has an internal structure: it is composed of a set of interrelated elements which may be modelled using entities and relationships.

When a view of an enterprise object is modified, the modification of all the related entities must be encapsulated in a single transaction because the partial execution of the modification would lead to an inconsistent status. More over, the other views describing the enterprise object will have to be updated if necessary.

The Design Specification Information View - Derivation process is very closely associated with the External to Root Schema Conversion Process. The steps in the derivation process provide a set of formulae which can be used to convert between the Run-Time External Schema and the Run-Time Root and Neuter Schema.

7.2.3 Components of the Information View

CIM-OSA Information building blocks are the elements which structure the enterprise information. In CIM-OSA the basic building blocks are related to the three Levels of genericity (Generic, Partial, and Particular). To indicate the genericity of the building blocks, the term type is associated with the building blocks at the different architectural Levels.

The conceptual schema is non-redundant, but open for extensions, as the enterprise does not need to be described completely in an one-time process, although it has to be described in depth for the analyzed parts.

Two classes of information building blocks have been defined:

Entity Building Blocks and **Relationship Building Blocks**.

Entity Building Blocks are :
- Group of Enterprise Object
- Enterprise Object
- View
- Information Element

The entity building blocks structure the information:
- Groups of Enterprise Objects contain Enterprise Objects
- Enterprise Objects contain Views
- Views contain Information Elements

Relationship building blocks are:
- Group to Group
- Group to Enterprise Object or Enterprise Object to Group
- Enterprise Object to Enterprise Object
- Enterprise Object to View or View to Enterprise Object
- View to View

Relationship building blocks are used to navigate through the information gathered by the Entity building blocks.

It is expected that a lot of view types will be defined for common disciplines such as mechanics, electronics, optics, software, logistics, etc.

The splitting of the conceptual schema into view types, allows abstraction of those view types which are sufficiently common to be hosted on the CIM-OSA Partial Level or even on the CIM-OSA Generic Level. Through these view types, the design of a Particular Requirements Definition Model will be greatly facilitated.

In addition to the information building blocks given above for the enterprise and Deign Specification Modelling Level some information building blocks have been defined for the Implementation Description Modelling Level. These building blocks model the Run Time aspects of information.

Run Time building blocks are:

> Editions
>> Variants
>> Transient
> Embodiments
> Detained and Disposable Views

These building blocks will support version management which is mainly concerned with edition control.

7.3 CIM-OSA Implementation Description Modelling Level Constructs

The abstract description of the IDPE requires a generic element that can be used to describe every distributed functionality. Following the OSI-approach, where 7 types of so called Entities are used (Layer 1: Physical Entity --- Layer 7: Application Entity) CIM-OSA introduces a generic construct called Functional Entity. The Functional Entity is an active element that can communicate with other Functional Entities. Graphically a total system can be described by a network of rectangles representing the Functional Entity Instances and Lines interconnecting them.

In CIM-OSA the Functional Entity construct is used to describe the behaviour of the Integrating Infrastructure IIS but also the specific functionality of the IDPE (outside the IIS).

The primary methods for communication between discrete processing elements of a distributed processing system are

- message passing: used in loosely coupled systems

- memory sharing: used in closely coupled systems

The memory sharing principle is often regarded as the more convenient way because it allows the software designer to organize the cooperation of software modules in tricky ways, in order to achieve optimum communication performance. The message passing principle however forces the designer to organize the complex functionality into autonomous areas which cooperate in a loosely coupled mode. This may sometimes appear inconvenient, but is the only way to organize distributable functionality safely.

7.3.1 Functional Entity Content

The Functional Entity Concept, including its transaction oriented style of cooperation, is close to the principles of object oriented processing. It is being applied in several areas of distributed Data Processing Standardisation.

The Functional Entity concept can also be based on the object oriented system modelling method. In this sense the Functional Entities (FE) can be considered to be Objects.

A set of FE with a common, characteristic, externally visible behaviour is referred to as an FE type. This behaviour of a FE type is divided into a set of unitary actions called type operations, each of which is distinct and logically complete. The operations are specified at a level of abstraction which defines what happens, not how it happens. The set of all behaviours of a FE type is completely defined by its set of type operations, and is referred to as its FE type specification. A FE type is referenced by its type name. All instances of a FE type have the same type operations. An instance is referenced specially by an instance name, and generically by its type name.

The type operation of a FE instance can be remotely called by other FE instances which may be of the same or different types. The complete interplay of calling an operation (request), performing the operation (action) and receiving the operation result (response) is here called a Transaction.

N.B: In object oriented programming the word class is often used in the same sense as Type. CIM-OSA favours for its Functional Entities the word Type, because this is more familiar in conventional data processing. Furthermore it should be noted that the adoption of the object oriented approach does not imply that the Functional Entities internal behaviour shall be implemented by use of object oriented languages.

The overall Implemented Functional Structure of real enterprises (both functions and control) possibly consists of thousand of Functional Entity Instances. To cope with this complexity, an overall Application System can be designed as a so called fractal hierarchy. This means that every Functional Entity can be decomposed into a network of more Elementary Functional Entities. This successive refinement procedure is repeated until Elementary Functional Entities are achieved that cannot be sensibly partitioned into sub-functions that exclusively communicate in a transaction oriented manner.

The internal functioning of the Elementary Functional Entity is then described and realized by Program Objects that can be executed by the planned resource type. For instance if a Functional Entity is to be implemented on a computer the description must be provided in an appropriate formal language. Implementation by a human being needs a description in natural language.

In CIM-OSA the Functional Entity paradigm is applied for the following purposes:

o   to describe the overall Implemented Functional View of the IDPE

o   to structure the Integrated Enterprise Operations (EOF) in terms of Implemented Functional Entities (IPF)

o   to structure the CIM-OSA Integrating Infra Structure IIS in terms of Services

o   the OSI-Communication environment which is made up of Layer-N-Entities is considered as a Functional Entity Structure

7.3.2 Functional Entity Communication

The Functional Entity is an implementation independent functional object able to send, receive, process (modify or interrogate) and optionally store information.

Communication between Functional Entities is transaction oriented. A Transaction is a single bidirectional exchange of messages from a requestor to its responding partner and from the responder to the requestor in that order. In detail the Transaction includes three sequential steps:

o   requestor sends a request data unit to the responder
o   responder acts upon the request
o   responder sends a response data unit to the requestor

In general the data units are structured types which can be called Protocol Data Units (PDU's). The entirety of Protocol Data Units agreed between two partners together with the Transaction oriented interaction rule is called Transaction Protocol. The set of Transactions defined between two Functional Entities is represented as a CHANNEL.

Figure 7-1 illustrates the generic behaviour of two interacting Functional Entities.

Both Entities have their own data that can only be accessed by their associated (virtual) processing facility. The data of a Functional Entity is generally referred to as its state, and the style of internal operation is called state oriented. However the internal functioning of a Functional Entity can be completely hidden from its partner. All capability is defined by the sets of Transaction Types provided at the Functional Entity Input/Output Channels.

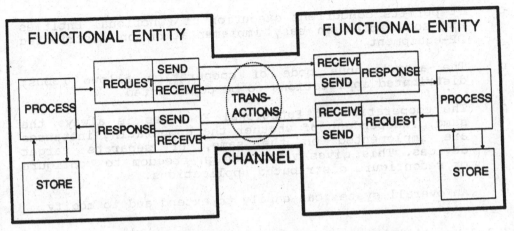

FUNCTIONAL ENTITIES can act as requestor, responder or both

FUNCTIONAL ENTITIES co-operate through TRANSACTIONS

A TRANSACTION includes three operations:
- Sending a request data unit from the requestor to the responder
- responders action upon the request
- sending a response data unit from the responder to the requestor

Figure 7-1: Behaviour of interacting Functional Entities

The activities of a Functional Entity always result in a request to be sent to a partner entity or in a response to be re-sent to a partner entity (upon a request sent by this partner).

Once a Functional Entity has received a request or a response data unit from a partner it takes full responsibility of this data. The partner then is unable to reaccess his issued data.

The exclusively local data access and the clearly defined interaction principle, has a number of advantages for functional design and implementation of information processing systems.

o   It enables (and forces) the designer to unambiguously assign responsibilities to autonomous functional objects. In this way each Functional Entity will represent an area of responsibility which it can control autonomously, and which does not need communication with other Functional Entities except such as can be modelled by asynchronous Transactions. This approach will lead to the production of well defined communicating software objects instead just pieces of code.

o   It permits concurrent execution of Functional Entities and so enables an easy implementation on distributed DP-equipment.

o   The asynchronous mode of cooperation allows robust distributed applications to be constructed.

o   The cooperation of Functional Entities is always the same, independent of whether the cooperating instances are implemented on the same, or separate target devices. This gives vital design freedom to configure or reconfigure distributed applications.

o   An overall system can easily to extend and to modify.

7.3.3 Functional Entities, Transactions, and Protocols

The functional capabilities of a Functional Entity are completely hidden for its cooperating partners. These capabilities are only visible through the set of Transactions, conveyed through their common channel, agreed upon between the partner Functional Entities.

Such Transaction Sets are defined by one or more **protocols**, which define the rules to be followed by communicating Functional Entities, each protocol defining a set of **Protocol Data Units** (PDUs).

The (Transaction) Protocols defined in the IDPE are categorized into three types:

    Access Protocol(s),
    Agent Protocol(s),
    External Protocol(s)

The Protocol Types used in the Integrating Infrastructure (IIS), and their Transaction Functional Unit Types, are defined in Section 7.4.

An example of a Transaction Functional Unit is the IFO Monitoring and Control Functional Unit (which controls an Implemented Functional Operation, IFO). It consists of the following set of Transactions:

    Start IFO
    Stop IFO
    Interrupt IFO
    Terminate IFO
    Restart IFO
    Abort IFO

7.4 CIM-OSA Integrating Infrastructure (IIS)

7.4.1 Concepts of the Architecture of the IDPE

To describe the CIM-OSA Integrating Infrastructure (IIS) Reference Model, the entire Integrated Data Processing Environment (IDPE) needs first to be described.

Everything outside the CIM-OSA Integrating Infrastructure is referred to as <u>external</u>.

7.4.1.1 The Functional Entity Construct

In the IDPE all active elements are called Functional Entities. As described in Section 7.3 the Functional Entity is a generic construct to describe distributed functions that cooperate by exchange of Protocol Data Units.

The IDPE is graphically described by one network diagram constructed of Functional Entities and Protocol Links. The graphical symbols and their use in a Functional Diagram are shown in Figure 7-2.

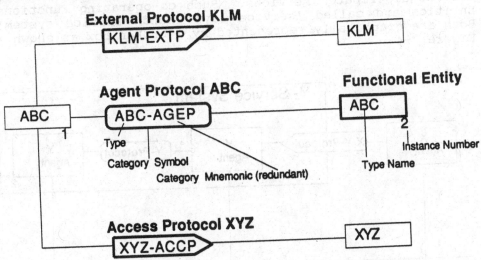

Figure 7-2: Graphical Symbols for Functional Diagrams

OSI defines a concept to implement the functions that are abstractly defined by a Functional Entity structure onto and layered service provided by another Functional Entity structure. These layered services can be accessed at a so called 'service interface'. In the IDPE Functional diagrams service interfaces are represented as arrows as depicted in Figure 7-3.

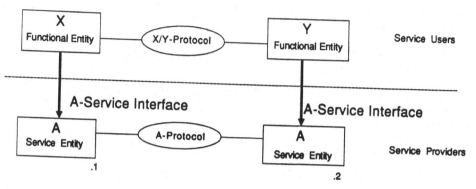

Figure 7-3: Graphical Representation of Service Interfaces

The interaction mechanism of Service Interfaces may differ from that of Protocol Links in the way that the Functional Entities may access the same variables in a common space of memory, where as a protocol link considers Protocol Data Units really exchanged between the protocol partners.

In the IDPE architectural concepts multiple Instances of the same Functional Entity Type may be combined in order to provide distributed services. Such co-operating Functional Entities are called 'service layer' and 'service system'. Both are graphically represented by a broken box as shown in Figure 7-4.

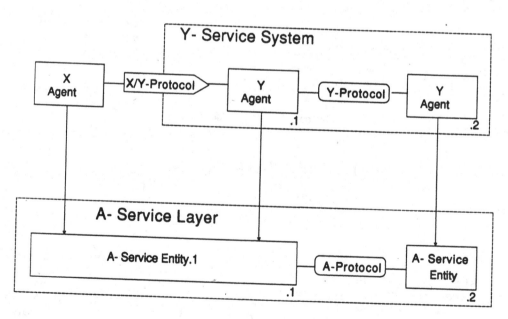

Figure 7-4: Graphical Representation of Service System and Service Layer

7.4.1.2 Layering Model

The Layering Model as defined in CIM-OSA is an adaptation of the ISO International Standard 7498 defining OSI. The model defines service interfaces and peer protocols. They are considered as a whole because service interfaces and peer protocols in that context are just two aspects of one global mechanism and they must be understood by reference to each other.

A Service (in the context of layering) is a capability of a service entity which is provided to other service entities or Functional Entities using the service at the boundary between the provider and the user entities.

A Peer Protocol is a set of rules and formats (semantic and syntactic) which determines the interworking behaviour of Entities of the same type in the performance of their functions. A Protocol consists of Protocol Data Units.

Services provided by a set of entities of the same type are built upon the peer protocol of that service. This protocol may in turn be implemented using a lower level service.

This possibility for a peer protocol to be implemented on a lower level service gives birth to an ordering of the layered services. Therefore, the terms (N)-service, (N-1)-service and the (N+1)-service, may be used to locate the relative positions of services, where N=1,2 .. L (Figure 7-5).

Entities of the uppermost layer of a layered architecture (N=L) do not provide a Service (e.g. in OSI the layer 7, application layer). Entities of the lowermost layer (N=1) do not use a Service.

Use of the Layering Model in the IIS

The Layering Model is used in the lower part of the IIS :

- all IIS defined protocols (except for those of System Wide Exchange and Communications Management) are implemented on the System Wide Exchange Service.

- The System Wide Exchange protocol is implemented on the services of Communications Management,

- The Communications Management protocol is implemented on the services of OSI (or other).

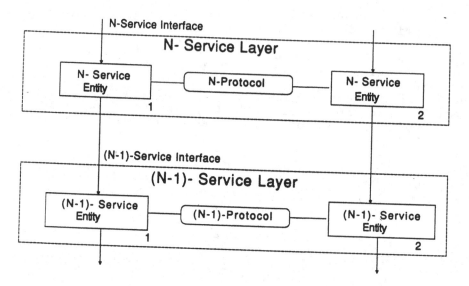

Figure 7-5: Layering Model

Remark:

The concept of layering is still under consideration. Since the evolving concept of OSI Application Layer Structure (ISO/DP9545, which is still under discussion) will not use any longer sub-layering in the application layer, the current thinking is to remove the layering concept from the ISS. Instead the required functions currently covered by System Wide Exchange and Communication Management shall be added as additional service elements to the Application Entity construct. It also has to be checked whether functions foreseen for IIS in general overlap with emerging international standards.

7.4.1.3 The Client-Service Model

The Client-Service Model is a generic architecture model which has already been introduced at least twice in:

- ISO DP 9072 Message Oriented Text Interchange Systems/Remote Operation Service/Part 1: concepts and Model, and

- ISO DP 9495/1 The Directory, Overview of Concepts, Models and Services.

The CIM-OSA use of the Client-Service Model has been based upon these sources.

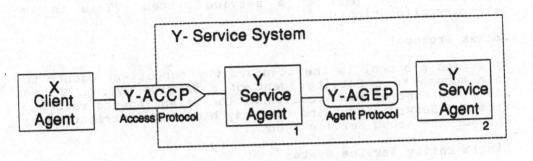

Figure 7-6: Functional Model of a Client-Service Relationship

The Client-Service Model (Figure 7-6) supposes a natural structuring of a distributed application into Functional Entities, some of which provide common services which are requested at need by the "client" Functional Entities.

Service System

A Service System is a complex, distributed functional entity that performs a set of basic and specific application services by means of Service Agents within the Service System. A Service Agent is a Functional Entity that provides services that can be requested by Clients Agents.

The set of services provided by a Service Agent are made visible to its Client Agents through an Access Protocol. This protocol is inherently asymmetric.

One or more Service Agents of the same type distributed through a network may interact to perform the requested service; in that case they cooperate by means of an Agent Protocol. Such interactions are not seen by the Client Agents of the Service Systems

Client System

A Client System is a system in which one or more Client Agents of one or more Service Systems reside.

A client agent is a functional entity that requests a service provided by a Service Agent.

Client/Service-Agent

This is a Functional Entity that may act as client agent and as Service Agent. Such combined Functional Entities are considered being part of a service system. (This is an arbitrary allocation).

Access Protocol

An access protocol is the standard way for client agents to gain access to a Service Agent of a Service System. It is the means that allows location of the Client Agents remotely from the Service Agent and that may hide the distribution of the Service among Service Agents.

Single Entity Service System

In some cases one may have to consider a Service System consisting of just one Service Agent. It still provides an Access Protocol but it has no Agent Protocol defined.

Application of the client-service model in the IIS

Entities of other types than System Wide Exchange and Communications Management have many client-service relationships among each other. These are described in Sections 7.4.3 to 7.4.12.

7.4.1.4 Linking the Client-Service Model with the Layering Model

The Access Protocol (see Figure 7-7) and the Agent Protocol of the entities observing the Client-Service Model are both implemented on the System Wide Exchange service which is the uppermost layered service defined in the IIS of CIM-OSA. Functional Entities outside the IIS (External Services) are accessed through External Protocols which are also implemented on System Wide Exchange (SE) Service. SE and CM are thereby used in a pass through mode.

7.4.2 Overview of the Resulting IDPE Architecture

From the functional point of view the Integrated Data Processing Environment (IDPE) can be divided into three major parts:

- the CIM-OSA Integrating Infra Structure (IIS) which supports the execution of all application specific functions

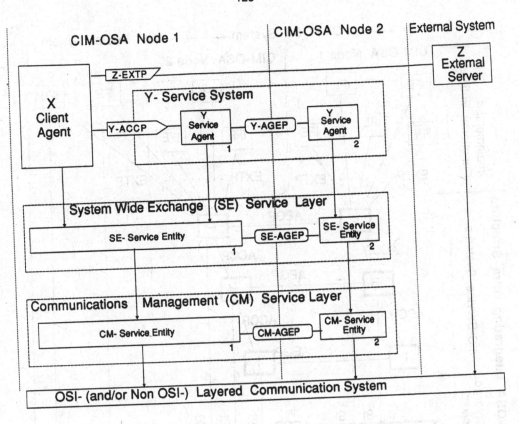

Figure 7-7: Linking the Client-Service Model with the Layering Model in the IIS

- clusters of application specific functions, so called Implemented Functional Entities (IFE). These represent all software components implemented to perform the enterprise Functional Operations (application programs, machine programs, CAD tools etc.)

- the functionality of the OSI environment which is preferably used to implement the communication requirements inside and outside the IIS.

The functional structure of these three areas of the IDPE is depicted in Figure 7-8. All boxes represent Functional Entities as described in Chapter 7.3.

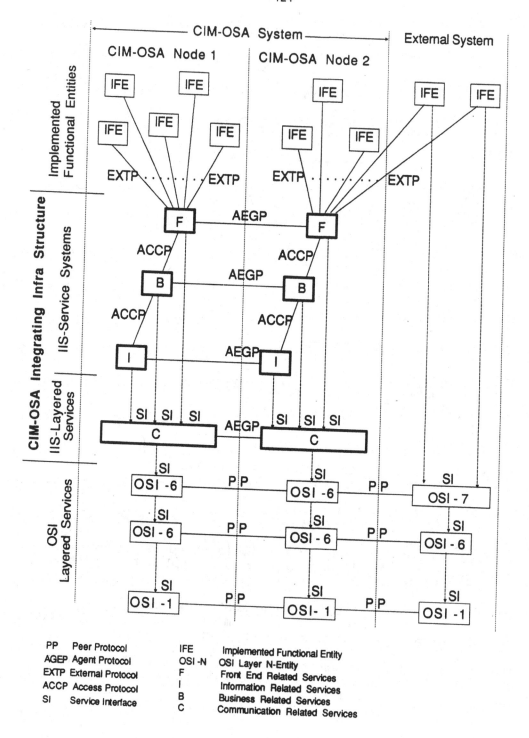

Figure 7-8: The Three Functional Areas of the IDPE

The Integrating Infrastructure is divided into four Types of Service-Complex:

-    Front End-Related Services (F)
-    Business-Related Services (B)
-    Information-Related Services (I)
-    Communication-Related Services (C)

An overall CIM-OSA System usually consists of several CIM-OSA Nodes. Each CIM-OSA Node may contain an Instance of each of the four Type of Service Complexes (F,B,I,C). Distributed instances of the same type form a so called Service System. Figure 7-8 exemplary shows a CIM-OSA system consisting of two CIM-OSA Nodes. For example the two Information Related Service Complexes (I) form the Information Related Service System which is to system wide provide services for information access, while taking care of consistency and integrity of system wide stored information entities. Accordingly Instances of the other three Service Complexes F, B and C form their distributed Service Systems.

The IIS Service Complexes are further subdivided into Services as shown in Figure 7-9 for one CIM-OSA Node. As pointed out in 7.4.1.2 and 7.4.1.3 two service concepts are used in the IIS:

-    Layering Model
-    Client-Service Model

Accordingly the IIS services are accessible through either

-    Access Protocols, or
-    a Service Interface

The services accessible through a service interface are grouped into the Communication Related Service Complex (C). The services of this Complex are:

-    Communications Management (CM), and
-    System Wide Exchange (SE).

Their purpose is to provide the System Wide Exchange service that is used for implementing the protocols that occur among services accessible through an access protocol and to enable the IIS to interface with different network architectures.

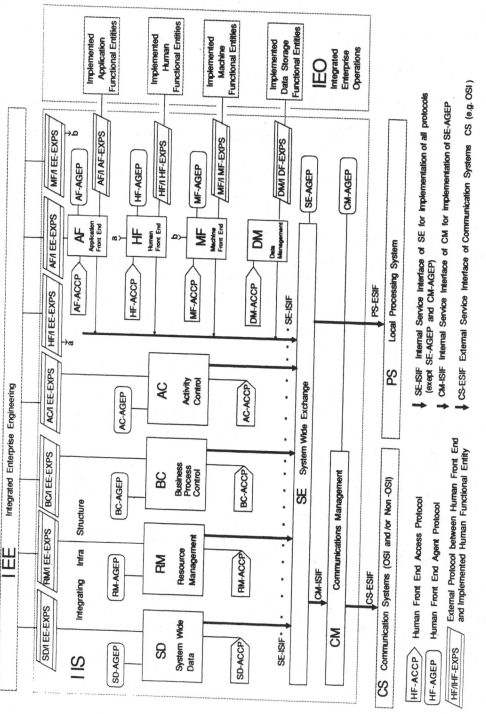

Figure 7-9: IDPE Overview

The C-Services are responsible for system wide homogeneous data communication. Their main purpose is to provide location independent data access, to establish transaction channels, to manage synchronized data transfer (broad cast, multicast), to perform data recording for recovery of pending requests. Thereby contributing to the reliability of data transfer. It is directly associated with basic communication services like OSI and others.

The services accessible through an access protocol are divided into three Service Complexes:

- Information related Services
- Front end related Services
- Business process related Services.

The information related services are:

- System Wide Data (SD)
- Data Management (DM).

Their purpose is, to provide data and information access protocols for their users, to gain a high level consistent Information. The I-Services contain functions to system wide store and retrieve and convert data. It also manages access rights, priority, integrity, redundancy and reliability of data handling.

The front end services are:

- Human Front End (HF),
- Machine Front End (MF), and
- Application Front End (AF).

Their purpose is to present to the Implemented External Functional Entities behind them (humans, machines and applications) the rest of the IDPE in a homogeneous fashion and conversely to present humans, machines and applications homogeneously to the rest of the IDPE.

In OSI-Terms the F-Services can be regarded as the CIM-OSA Application Interface to all external device specific functions. It provides the capability of all external data processing functions in a homogeneous form, namely as Functional Entities as defined in chapter 7.3. This means, any specific interaction method with external functional objects (Application Programs, Machine Programs etc.) is translated into the transaction oriented interaction behaviour. The Front End Related Services also allow to dynamically configure the external (outside the IIS) data processing system. Both physical equipment (machines, people) and programs are in a set up process arranged to accomplish the Implemented Functional Entities that can perform the Implemented Functional Operations defined in the

CIM-OSA Implementation Description Model (Function View and Resource View, see Figures 5-12 and 5-15).

The business process related services are:

- Activity Control (AC),
- Resource Management (RM), and
- Business Process Control (BC).

The purpose of these services is:

- to provide a higher level of stability of the applications by isolating them from the impact of organisational changes and control functions. This reduces the maintenance effort for applications,

- to provide a link between the CIM-OSA modelling environment, the Integrated Enterprise Engineering Environment (IEEE), the CIM-OSA operational environment and the Integrated Enterprise Operational Environment (IEOE),

  o by using the released Implemented Function View containing the Implemented Procedural Rule Sets and the relevant Implemented Functional Operations (see Figure 5-12),

  o by using the released Implemented Resource View and the released Implemented Organisation View (see Figure 5-15),

  o by supporting the orderly release of changes in the implementation to the operational level of the enterprise,

- to provide a defined set of facilities for consistent system wide management of the execution of Business Processes and Enterprise Activities and of the resources they use,

- to provide a logical link from the Implementation Description Model to the Implemented External Functional Entities performing the Enterprise Activities through the request of Implemented Functional Operations.

The detailed description of all the IIS services is given in the following Sections. The generic structure of each service description is the following:

Purpose of the Service
Functions of the Service divided into Functional Units
Access Protocols used (of other Services)
Access Protocols provided (to other Services)

Agent Protocols (for cooperation of Service Agents within a Service System)
External Protocols (agreed with External Functional Entities)
Layered Services used
Layered Services provided

7.4.3 Communications Management (CM) Service

The Communications Management is a Service of the Integrating Infra-Structure (IIS) defined by CIM-Open System Architecture/Integrated Data Processing Environment (CIM-OSA/IDPE).

This Service is based on the concepts developed in the Basic Reference Model for Open Systems Interconnection (ISO 7498).

7.4.3.1 Purpose

The Communications Management can be considered as a layered Service and supports the System Wide Exchange (SE)-Service by providing the mechanism for message transfer between CIM-OSA Services on different CIM-OSA nodes, or CIM-OSA node and non CIM-OSA node.

The Communications Management provides the Communications Management Services for the purpose of implementing the Access-, Agent- and External Protocols derived by System Wide Exchange (SE) to Services within Remote Nodes.

It provides a means for the CIM-OSA Services to access the **transparently** OSI Environment or the private Communication Environment and enables the transfer of information using real communication system (CS).

One major point of the Communications Management is to select which Communication Service is responsible for the establishment of the Information Transfer on CIM-OSA nodes.

7.4.3.2 Functions Within Communications Management

The Communications Management contains the functions which coordinate, control and maintain the Communication Handling between CIM-OSA nodes or CIM-OSA node and non CIM-OSA node.

Those Functions can be structured internally into groups of functions:

- **CM-Identify**

  o identifies and controls incoming message
  o checks to ensure the validity of this message
  o selects relevant communication resources
  o carries out message transfer using these selected resources

- **CM-Configuration**

  o identifies, collects and keeps records of all kind of communication resources from and to Communications Management Information Base (CM-View)
  o performs mapping of Communications Management Services required by other CIM-OSA Services onto either OSI Services or non OSI (private) Services in external Communication Server.

- **CM-Synchronization**

  Controls a timely access of CIM-OSA Services to the communication resources for the purpose of the Information Transfer.

7.4.3.3 Overview of Functions and Layered Services

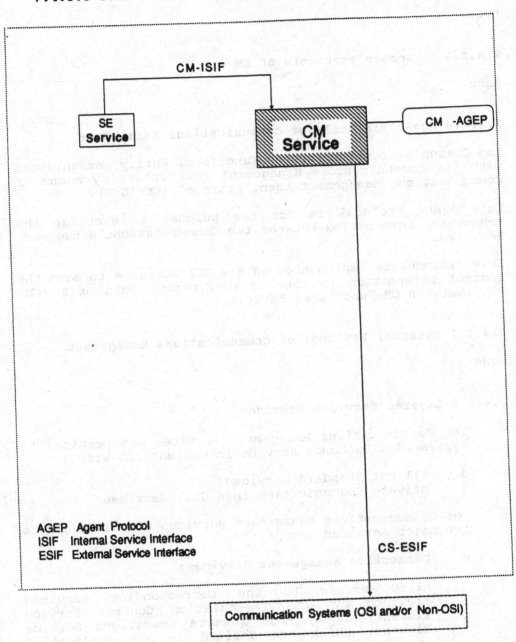

Figure 7-10: Protocols and Layered Services used and
provided by Communication Management

7.4.3.4   Access Protocols used

7.4.3.5   Access Protocols of CM

7.4.3.6 Agent Protocols of Communications Management

The Communications Management Functional Entity communicates with its Communications Management Peer entity by means of Communications Management Agent Protocol (CM-AGEP).

This Agent Protocol is for the purpose to exchange the Management Information between two Communications Management Services.

This Protocol is implemented on the OSI Services to pass the Control Information in form of CM-Protocol Data Unit (CM-PDU) between CM-Functional Entities.

7.4.3.7 External Protocol of Communications Management

7.4.3.8 Layered Services Provided

-    The Communications Management Services are provided to System Wide Exchange Service in conjunction with :

     o   all OSI Standard Services
     o   private Communication (non OSI) Services

-    The Communications Management Services are divided into two major Services groups :

     o   **Connection Management Services:**

          allow access to the corresponding services provided by ACSE (Association Control Service Element) or by ROSE (Remote Operations Service Element) which are defined in the Application Layer of the OSI standard services for the purpose of the Control of the Application Association.

There are the following Services:

- CM-ASSOCIATE
- CM-RELEASE
- CM-ABORT

These Services allow the CM-User to initialise, associate, release or abort the communication between nodes.

o   **Application Management Services:**

allow access to the corresponding services provided by SASE (Specific Application Service Element) in the Application Layer of the OSI Reference Model or provided by proprietary (non OSI) services for the purpose of the operation of the CIM-OSA Functional Entities.

The following services are defined:

- CM-DATA-TRANSFER-OPERATION
- CM-STATUS-OPERATION
- CM-DIRECTORY-OPERATION
- CM-JOB-CONTROL-OPERATION
- CM-PROGRAM-LOAD-OPERATION
- CM-VARIABLE-OPERATION
- CM-FILE-OPERATION
- CM-BROADCAST-OPERATION

7.4.3.9 Layered Services Used

- OSI services
- private communication services

7.4.4 The System Wide Exchange (SE) Service

7.4.4.1 Purpose

The purpose of the System Wide Exchange Service is to:

- provide the adequate service needed to implement access, agent, and external protocols occurring among data oriented services, activity control oriented services and front end services,
- enable its service users to remain unconcerned with the notion of CIM-OSA Node and thence with any networking issue and to know their correspondents only as IIS Services Entities,
- factor out the majority of concerns for reliability engineering,

- factor out as many as possible of the issues of asynchronous communication.

7.4.4.2 Functions of System Wide Exchange

System Wide Exchange is a layered service and performs the following functions:

- Service entity locating that is: the mapping of system wide unique application entity identifiers onto CIM-OSA nodes.
- Accept (and record and refer in later use) lists of correspondent entities which a user entity may wish to use. Use these list upon request by the user.
- Asynchronous transmission: when a receiver entity is unable (down, busy, ...) to accept a PDU that is addressed to it, and depending on mode parameters, System Wide Exchange will convey the PDU to it later with periodical further attempts. It will report appropriately on this to the service requestor.
- Reliability engineering: tracking of pending requests, etc.
- Initiate selection of application entity requested communication service in Communications Management, by providing service access points and/or copying the PDU flag from the protocol of the requesting service into the SE protocol, for the purpose of all relevant information being on the outside envelope of the PDU for processing.
- Translate client/service application entity "names" into real node/application entity addresses (of Service Access Points).
- Access to local devices is currently being handled by the proprietary implementation of the system, waiting for standards in this domain.

7.4.4.3 Overview of Protocols and Layered Services

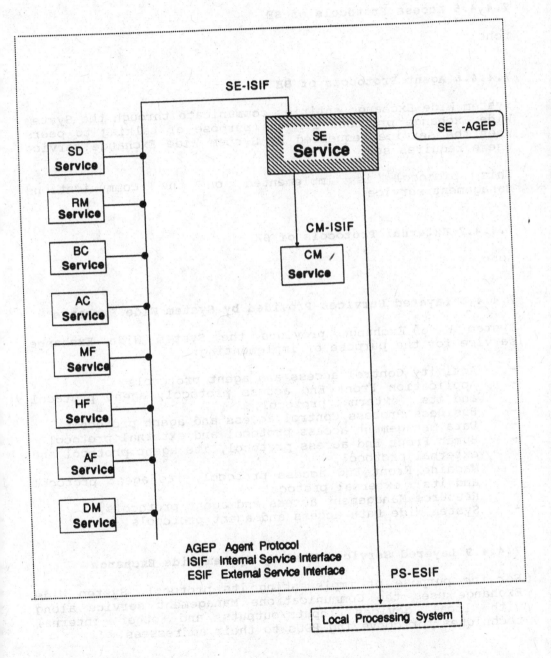

Figure 7-11: Protocols and Layered Services used and provided by System Wide Exchange

7.4.4.4 Access Protocols Used

7.4.4.5 Access Protocols of SE

7.4.4.6 Agent Protocols of SE

System Wide Exchange entities communicate through the System Wide Exchange protocol for the purpose of talking to peers when the service requested by System Wide Exchange service users requires so.

This protocol is implemented on the Communications Management service.

7.4.4.7 External Protocols of SE

7.4.4.8 Layered Services Provided by System Wide Exchange

System Wide Exchange provides the System Wide Exchange service for the purpose of implementing:

- Activity Control access and agent protocols,
- Application Front End access protocol, agent protocol and its external protocol,
- Business Process Control access and agent protocols,
- Data Management access protocol and external protocol
- Human Front End access protocol, its agent protocol and external protocol,
- Machine Front End access protocol, its agent protocol and its external protocol
- Resource Management access and agent protocols,
- System Wide Data access and agent protocols.

7.4.4.9 Layered Services Used by System Wide Exchange

For the purpose of implementing its protocol, System Wide Exchange uses the Communications Management service along with local devices inputs/outputs and other internal techniques for conveying PDUs to their addressees.

7.4.5 The System Wide Data (SD) Service

7.4.5.1 Purpose

The purpose of the System Wide Data Service is to:

- provide a system wide data access to its clients,
- provide the data the clients request in the schema they specify or in a negotiated schema acceptable to them, whatever the actual storage schema is,
- enable its clients to remain ignorant of actual data distribution and redundancy when they apply,
- allow access to data only to duly authorized requestors,
- maintain system wide data and information integrity according to systems rule,
- perform efficiently as a data and information service.

7.4.5.2 Functions of System Wide Data

System Wide Data is a multiple entity service system and performs the following functions:

- data access rights,
- segment/reassemble data request,
- system wide data consistency,
- data schema conversions (System Wide Data performs it itself or monitors its performance within other Services),
- data location (determine in which Storage group(s) the data to be written must be put or from which one the requested data must be fetched),
- selection of Storage Group to retrieve from when several contain the requested data,
- allocation of storage group(s) where to store new data.

In addition, the following information management functions fall into System Wide Data Service:

- provide identifiers
- context definition,
- Configuration Item linkage to context,
- context switching,
- context resolution,
- Configuration Item absolute name to Configuration Item identifier,

7.4.5.3 Overview of Protocols and Layered Services

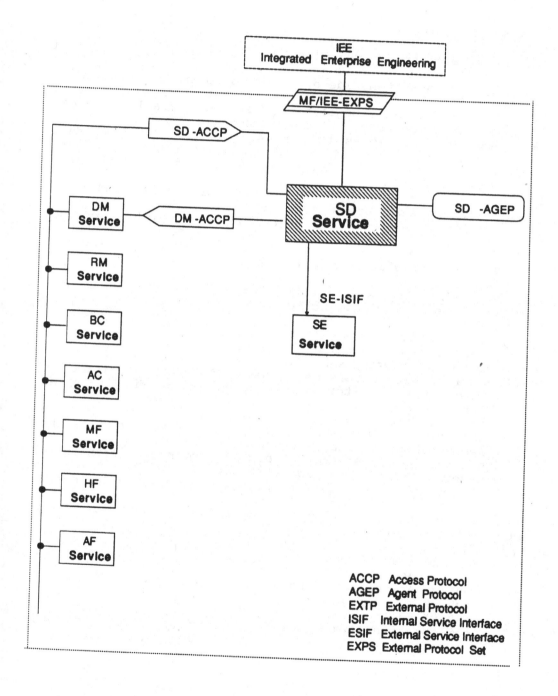

Figure 7-12: Protocols and Layered Services used and provided by System Wide Data

7.4.5.4 Access Protocols Used by System Wide Data

System Wide Data uses the following services:

- Data Management service for the purpose of:
  - o fetching data location information. This information is contained in a Storage Group which System Wide Data already knows.
  - o accessing the data requested by clients after it has been located.
- a subset of the Machine Front End service built on its "Machine data input and output" Functional Unit, for the purpose of guaranteeing system wide consistent updates of NC control programs.
- similar subsets of the Application Front End and Human Front End services for similar reasons,
- the Application Front End services for the purpose of invoking non standard schemas converters.

7.4.5.5 Access Protocol of System Wide Data

System Wide Data provides the System Wide Data access protocol to its clients for them to benefit from the system wide integrated data service.

This protocol is implemented on the System Wide Exchange service.

7.4.5.6 Agent Protocol of System Wide Data

System Wide Data entities communicate through the System Wide Data agent protocol for the purpose of :

- subcontracting to peers the locating of data (this can take the form of polling Data Centres or other techniques). This protocol is implemented on the System Wide Exchange service.
- for communication between two or more peer entities of Data Centres.

7.4.5.7 External Protocol of System Wide Data

System Wide Data entities communicate with the Integrated Enterprise Engineering (IEE) through the SD/IEE External Protocol for the purpose of providing to it the system wide integrated data services.

7.4.5.8 Layered Services Provided by System Wide Data

7.4.5.9 Layered Services Used by System Wide Data

System Wide Data uses System Wide Exchange service for the purpose of implementing its access and agent protocols.

7.4.6 The Data Management (DM) Service

7.4.6.1 Purpose

The purpose of the Data Management Service is to:

- provide local data storage and retrieval to be used in association with System Wide Data,
- enable the insertion into CIM-OSA systems of DBMSs or other means of data storage in a standardised fashion.

7.4.6.2 Functions of Data Management

Data Management is a single entity server system and performs the following functions:

- Local store/retrieve, including manufacturing specific parameters defined in CIM-OSA such as: view edition,
- Serialisation of local data requests addressed to it,
- Storage Group Identifiers mapping onto data sets and data sets identifiers,
- Addressing in Storage Group,
- Data consistency within Storage Group. This includes the ability to be a partner in distributed commitment or other modes of data consistency enforcement.
- Schema conversions (complementing the same function within System Wide Data and subject to schema negotiation with System Wide Data.

7.4.6.3 Overview of Protocols and Layered Services

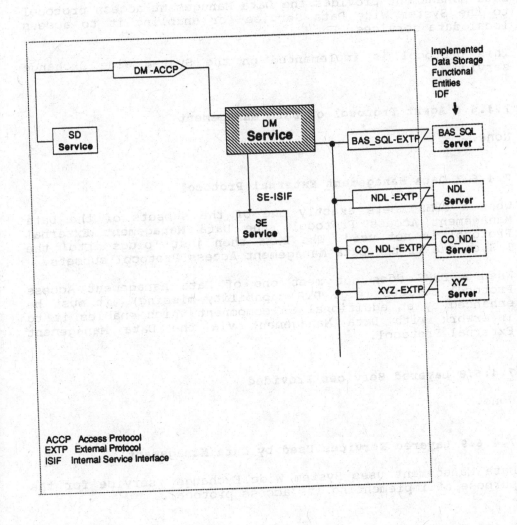

ACCP   Access Protocol
EXTP   External Protocol
ISIF   Internal Service Interface

Figure 7-13: Protocols and Layered Services used and
provided by Data Management

7.4.6.4 Access Protocols Used by Data Management

None.

7.4.6.5 Access Protocol of Data Management

Data Management provides the Data Management access protocol to the System Wide Data Service for enabling it to access local data services.

This protocol is implemented on the System Wide Exchange service.

7.4.6.6 Agent Protocol of Data Management

None.

7.4.6.7 Data Management External Protocol

When a DBMS meets exactly one of the subsets of the Data Management Access Protocol, the Data Management External Protocol is not used. The DBMS then just 'plugs into' the IIS on one of the Data Management Access Protocol subsets.

When a DBMS does not meet one of Data Management Access Protocol subsets (e.g. DTP capability missing), it must be enhanced by an additional SW component which enables it to interwork with Data Management via the Data Management External Protocol.

7.4.6.8 Layered Services Provided

None.

7.4.6.9 Layered Services Used by Data Management

Data Management uses System Wide Exchange service for the purpose of implementing its access protocol.

7.4.7 The Machine Front End Service

7.4.7.1 Purpose

The main purpose of the Machine Front End Service is to represent external data processing equipment such as Numeric Controllers, Robot Controllers, Programmable Controllers, etc. within a CIM-OSA Node in a homogeneous way.

In the IIS of a CIM-OSA Node the Machine Front End Service is manifested by an Instance of the Functional Entity Type MACHINE FRONT END.

Each CIM-OSA Node may contain zero or one Machine Front End Instance. It is a CIM-OSA System design decision whether a CIM-OSA Node is equipped with a Machine Front End Instance or not. Normally those CIM-OSA Nodes that are directly concerned with coordinating control of machines (robots, machine tools etc.) will be equipped with a Machine Front End. Examples for those Nodes are Cell-Controller Nodes or Shop Controller Nodes.

In the CIM-OSA Implementation Description Model all machine specific functionality is abstractly described by types of the category of Implemented Machine Functional Entities (IMF) which belongs to the category of Implemented Productive Functional Entities (IPF).

A Machine Functional Entity Type is capable to perform one or more types of Implemented Machine Functional Operations (IMO) (Category of the category of Implemented Functional Operations IFO).

Each Machine Front End Instance is responsible for one or more Implemented Machine Functional Entity Instances and consequently for one or more Implemented Machine Functional Operation Instances.

Within the Machine Front End each Implemented Machine Functional Operation (IMO) Instance is manifested in an Implemented Machine Functional Operation Controller (IMO-Controller).

The IMO Controllers allow the Machine Front End Users (normally Activity Control) to monitor and control the Implemented Machine Functional Operations (IMO). The IMO Controller is a configurable element that allows the Front End designer to complement each particular functional object (eg. a machine program) in such a way that it behaves as the CIM-OSA Implemented Machine Functional Operation. The set of IMO-Controllers constitute the configurable Application Interface for the interaction with remote machines.

Each IMO Controller provides a set of functions (e.g. START, STOP, RESTART etc.) that can be called by the Front End clients (normally Activity Control and Resource Management).

7.4.7.2 Functions Within Machine Front End

Machine Front End Set-Up Functional Unit

Before a Machine Functional Entity can be asked to execute IMO,s it has to be installed. This is to be performed in the following way.

In an initial state the Machine Front End knows neither Machine Devices nor Implemented Machine Functional Entities. It just contains the following Machine Front End Supporting Functions.

- Device Monitoring and Control. This Function performs device specific tasks such as power on, emergency stop, providing of the Device Status Report etc.

- Machine Device Installer. This Function is invoked by Activity Control or Human Front End in order to install particular Machine Device Controllers for each Device that the Machine Front End shall take responsibility of. After installation of a Machine Device Controller the respective Device can be handled by the Device Monitoring and Control Unit.

- Machine Functional Entity Installer. This Function is invoked by Activity Control or by a Human via a Human Front End in order to create a Machine Functional Entity Instance. This includes measures such as:

  - acquire Device Instance
  - load IMO Controllers into Machine Front End
  - load Machine Program into Machine Control Device
  - supply control parameters

7.4.7.2.1 Implemented Machine Functional Operation (IMO) Monitoring and Control Functional Unit

An Implemented Machine Functional Entity Instance is able to perform one or more Machine Functional Operation Instances, which may be of different Type. There are two classes of Machine Functional Operation Types

- Parallel Operations which can be carried out concurrently.
- Sequential Operations that can only be performed one after the other because they need the same instance of a physical element.

Each Machine Functional Operation Instance can be invoked multiply (subsequently) at definite occasions. Such a particular event is called a Machine Operation Occasion.

Implemented Machine Functional Operation (IMO) Instances are the objects that can individually be addressed and called for execution by clients (normally Business Process Management.) IMOs are manifested in the Machine Front End as installed IMO-Controllers. These can be invoked through a set of Transactions (such as START, STOP, RESTART, etc.)

7.4.7.2.2 Machine Functional Entity Data Input/Output Functional Unit

This Functional Unit includes functions to exchange at execution time parameter and variable values between Implemented Machine Functional Entities and IIS Functional Entities acting as clients (normally BC, AC and HF).

7.4.7.2.3 Machine Device Directory Report Functional Unit

The purpose of this Functional Unit is to inform clients of Machine Front End about

- system wide available Machine Devices
- static information objects stored in external devices data stores (e.g. in an MMS virtual file store)
- dynamic information subjects such as loaded (executable and executing) programs, libraries etc. (e.g. the content of an MMS-VMD-Domain)

The Functional Unit also allows to rename but not to delete or insert objects. This kind of configuration management measures are supported by the Machine Device Set Up Functional Unit.

7.4.7.2.4 Machine Functional Entity Diagnosis Functional Unit

This Functional Unit provides functions for animation and observation of executing Implemented Machine Functional Entities for the purpose of diagnosis and trouble shooting. This includes the following function:

- Get information of installed capability both device oriented and function oriented, e.g. device configuration, data structures and functional structures.

- Set up of test configurations such as alarm conditions, trigger conditions, journals, test input generator.

- Handling of the test configuration as for instance: Domination of control, notify and acknowledge alarm, start, interrupt and stop test sequences.

The functions of this Functional Unit are normally used by Human Front End.

7.4.7.2.5 Resource Management Supporting Functional Unit

The Functions provided by this Unit are to help the Resource Management Service to accomplish its machine specific management task. The Functional Unit provides Functions to arrange on behalf of Resource Management assignment and reservation of Machine Devices and to inform about their actual and expected status.

7.4.7.3 Overview of Protocols and Layered Services

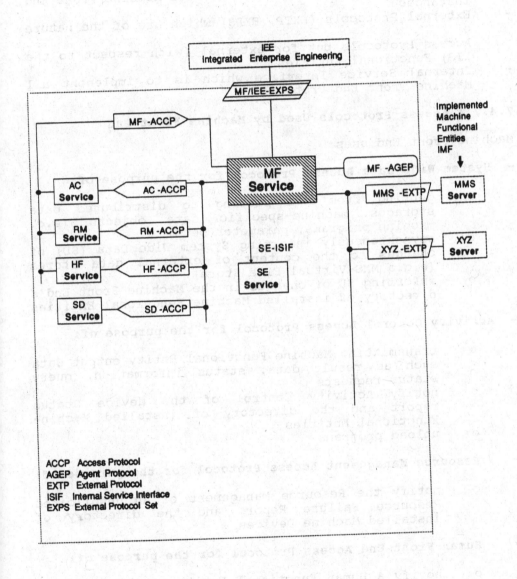

ACCP Access Protocol
AGEP Agent Protocol
EXTP External Protocol
ISIF Internal Service Interface
EXPS External Protocol Set

Figure 7-14: Protocols and Layered Services used and provided by the Machine Front End

Figure 7-14 shows the relationships of the Machine Front End Service Agent to other IIS Functional Entities. There are 4 categories of relationships.

- Access Protocols (ACCP) to access Services of the IIS Service Agents
- Agent Protocols (AGEP) agreed between Machine Front End Instances
- External Protocols (EXTP, EXPS) which are of the nature of

  Access Protocols but for external (with respect to the IIS) Functional Entities
- Internal Service Interface which is to implement all Machine Front End Protocols.

7.4.7.4 Access Protocols Used by Machine Front End

Machine Front End uses:

- **System Wide Data Access Protocol for the purpose of:**

  o getting from and putting to distributed data storages machine-specific data objects (e.g. machine programs, parameter sets)

  o asynchronously informing System Wide Data (SD) of changes to the content of external data stores (e.g.a MMS-Virtual File Store)

  o informing SD of changes in the Machine Front End's directory of installed Machine Functional Entities

- **Activity Control Access Protocol for the purpose of:**

  o transmitting Machine Functional Entity output data such as result data, status information, query status requests

  o notify Activity Control of the device Status report and the directory of installed Machine Functional Entities

  o upload programs

- **Resource Management Access Protocol for the purpose of:**

  o notify the Resource Management of an unsolicited Resource Failure Report and the directory of installed Machine Devices

- **Human Front End Access Protocol for the purpose of:**

  o notify a Human Functional Entity of alarm, status of Machine Functional Entities and Machine Devices

7.4.7.5 Access Protocol of Machine Front End

Machine Front End provides the Machine Front End Access Protocol to its clients for them to benefit homogeneous access to external machine specific devices. This protocol allows to:

- acquire, reserve, query status of Machine Devices
- define, set up, parameterise Machine Functional Entities
- control, data input, data output, query status of Machine

Functional Entities

- Diagnose Machine Devices
- Diagnose Machine Functional Entities

7.4.7.6 Agent Protocol of Machine Front End

Machine Front End Entities communicate through the Machine Front End Agent Protocol for the purpose of:

- Multicast configuration information among the Machine Front End Entities of the Machine Front End Service System. This is to provide in each Machine Front End entity an actual list of system wide available Machine Devices.

- Use Machine Devices that are managed by different Machine Front End Entities to support one Machine Functional Entity.

- Interconnect different Machine Functional Entities defined in two or more Machine Front End Entities for the Purpose of cooperation or coordination.

7.4.7.7 External Protocols Used by Machine Front End

7.4.7.7.1 External Protocol between Machine Front End and Implemented Machine Functional Entities

Communication Partners of the Machine Front End are Implemented External Functional Entities of the Category Implemented Machine Functional Entity IMF. An IMF is the abstract description of the functional capability of Machine Devices (MD) which consists of

- Mechanical Machine Device (MMD)
- Machine Control Device (MCD)
- Machine Device Agent (if required) (MDA)

It is assumed that an IMF always acts as a Server. Client is a Machine Front End Entity.

If there are standardised Services that define the interaction of machine specific clients and servers, the access protocols of such client server relationships are adopted by the CIM-OSA Machine Front End. Because such protocols are specified outside the IIS they are called External Protocols. Currently the MMS Protocol including the device specific Companion Standards is adopted as a CIM-OSA External Protocol.

Other emerging device specific communication standards can be adopted. Communication with Devices using a protocol not adopted by CIM-OSA may be connected by means of external Machine Device Agents (Protocol converters, gateways).

Machine Specific External Protocols are implemented on System Wide Exchange Service (SE), which uses in turn either the Communications Management (CM) Service in the case of remote Devices or the Local Processing Service (External Service Interface) in the case of locally attached Devices. Since the communication architecture of external Nodes do not provide SE and CM, these IIS Service Layers are used in a pass through mode.

7.4.7.7.2 External Protocol between Machine Front End and Integrated Enterprise Engineering IEE

MF communicates through the MF/IEE External Protocols for the Purpose introducing the relevant functional components of the Implementation mode.

7.4.7.8 Layered Services Provided by Machine Front End

7.4.7.9 Layered Services Used by Machine Front End

The Machine Front End uses the services of System Wide Exchange to implement its access protocols, its agent protocols and its external protocols.

7.4.8 The Human Front End (HF) Service

7.4.8.1 Purpose

The purpose of the Human Front End is to mediate between the human user and the CIM-OSA system. The HF has to be consistent, implementation and application independent. In standard systems of today the user interface is the intermediary between human user and system. It is part of the application programs and thus application and implementation dependent.

To change this situation in CIM-OSA systems the kernel functionality of the user interface must be separated from the application programs and from the device dependent parts. This kernel functionality then is called the HF. The HF thus mediates between the rest of the Integrating Infrastructure (the standardised CIM specific parts of the former application programs) and the future specific application programs on one side and the Implemented Human Functional Entities on the other side (see Figure 7-15). The HF communicates with the rest of the CIM-OSA system and application programs via a set of access protocols and with the implemented human functional entities via a set of external protocols.

The Implemented Human Functional entities (IHF) comprise the operational human users, the interaction devices, the device control (device drivers etc.) and the device agents which perform as far as necessary the network services and protocol conversions between the external protocol of the HF and the special device protocols, etc.

To fulfil it`s goals the concept of the HF is based on the relevant results of the modern research activities in the user interface field:

- architectural concepts of User Interface Management Systems
- software ergonomics concepts from Human Factors Activities
- graphics standards
- concurrency and network connectivity from modern Window Management Systems

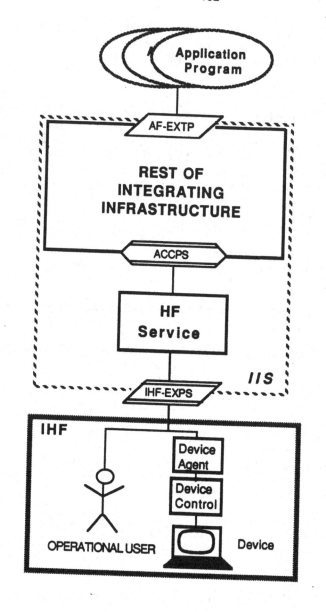

IIS	Integrating Infrastructure
HF	Human Front End
IHF	Implemented Human Functional Entity
ACCPS	Access Protocol Set from the HF and the rest of the IIS
AP-EXTP	External Protocol between HF and Applications Programs
IHF-EXTPS	External Protocol Set between HF and IHF

Figure 7-15: Human Front End as part of the CIM-OSA
Integrating Infrastructure

With this concept the HF enables the human user to interact with a CIM-OSA system in a homogeneous way independent of the connected application programs. And it enables the CIM-OSA system to communicate with different users via different interaction devices homogeneously.

7.4.8.2 Functions Within Human Front End

7.4.8.2.1 Functional Structure of Human Front End

Figure 7-16 shows the functional structure of the Human Front End.

The HF contains 3 main functional building blocks

- Interaction Management
- Presentation Management
- Application Interface Management

which provide the necessary functionality.

The required application and device independence of this functionality demands the intermediary between any used application program and any Implemented Human Functional Entity. This is only possible if the HF has knowledge of both sides. This knowledge must be contained in a set of Operational Models. These Operational Models are part of the released Implementation Description Model of the enterprise.

The set of Operational Models contains:

Application Interface Models which contain descriptions of the functionality of the programs and of the necessary inputs and outputs, so that the HF is able to present outputs from the programs to the user in an understandable way (add information as clear text, help information etc.) and to enable the HF to ask the user for inputs and check his inputs.

Interaction models which contain interaction styles defined during the model building process.

User models which contain the user profiles (capabilities, experience, preferences concerning interaction styles etc.) and the user responsibilities in the enterprise (as part of the Organisation Model).

Device models which contain the functional description of the defined logical devices and the categorisation of the available physical devices.

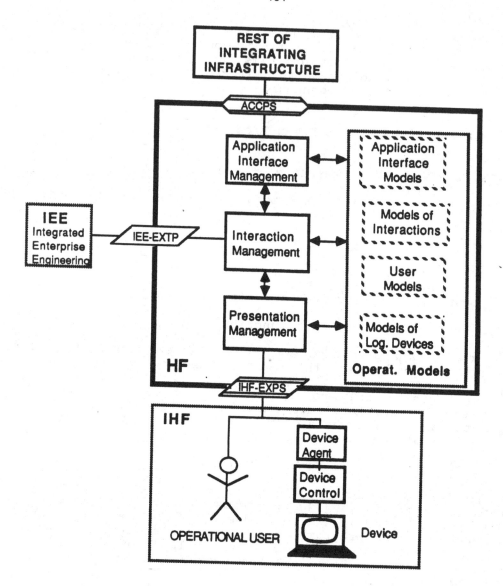

HF	Human Front End
IHF	Implemented Human Functional Entity
ACCPS	Access Protocol Set from the HF and the rest of the Integrating Infrastructure
IHF-EXPS	External Protocol Set between HF and IHF
ISE-EXTP	External Protocol between HF and IEE

Figure 7-16: Internal Structure of Human Front End

Parts of the functions of the HF are accessible from outside the HF through the different protocols. These 'visible' functions can be divided into 3 groups

- Basic HF functions
- HF functions related to services of the Integrated Infrastructure
- HF functions related to application programs

The following paragraphs describe the different functional units.

7.4.8.2.2 Interaction Management

The Interaction Management as central part of the HF defines the syntax of the dialogue between the user and the application.

It handles the flow of control in the dialogue and decides on the next action to be initiated (event handling).

It selects the interaction styles depending on the Implementation Description Model (user model, application interface model, interaction model, device model) and the system state and controls them during operation.

The Interaction Management functional unit controls which logical devices should be enabled. It determines acceptable logical inputs for the current state of the dialogue, determines correctness of inputs and generates echoing of inputs.

If the Integrated Enterprise Engineering delivers new releases of used Operational Models, the exchange of these models is controlled by Interaction Management.

7.4.8.2.3 Presentation Management

The presentation Management functional unit controls the external appearance of the HF.

It controls the logical to physical device bindings.

It translates from internal abstract output descriptions to the external representation and from the actual input to internal abstract representation (external protocol).

It contains functions like:

- Display Management

    This functionality controls and enables the delivery of the information to the user on the virtual output devices involved (e.g. what should be displayed where, what does the menu look like etc.).

- Window Management

    The window manager controls the connection between application processes and windows (virtual devices) and the size and placement of windows.

    The management of the different windows on a physical device is done outside the Integrating Infrastructure by the basic window manager or window server which is device dependent and will be implemented as part of the device agent (Figure 7-16).

    The combined functionality of the window manager of the HF and of the outside window server enables the user to view multiple sources of information and handle multiple tasks simultaneously (e.g. presentation of the same information in different windows for different purposes, ability to view and interact with different application processes in different windows on the same device) and enables Integrating Infrastructure services or application programs to present information on different virtual devices (windows) at the same time.

7.4.8.2.4 Application Interface Management

The services of the Integrating Infrastructure and the application programs are performing application processes. Thus the interface between the HF and the rest of the IIS can be seen as the application interface. This interface is managed by the Application Interface Management functional unit.

The Application Interface Management functional unit converts requests from the other services of the Integrating Infrastructure into internal events to be handled by the Interaction Manager and builds requests to the other services.

Via the Application Front End the Application Interface Management has to communicate with the used application programs. To be able to do so the Application Interface Management needs to know about the input and output parameters of the applications as well as of their effects.

To get this knowledge, it uses the application interface model.

7.4.8.2.5 Basic HF Functions

This group of functions comprises basic functions of a modern user interface which are independent of the application for which they are used.

Typical functions are:

- Start-up
- Text Editing
- Graphics Editing
- Local Undo/Redo
- Local Help
- Configuration Dialogue

7.4.8.2.6 HF Functions related to services of the Integrated Infrastructure

This set of functions contains the specific functionality for the realization of the interaction between human user and the other Integrating Infrastructure services.

Typical functions of this group are:

- presentation of the functionality of the Integrating Infrastructure to the user in a way that the user can understand it by adding available information dependent on the user profile etc.
- monitoring of the status of the Integrating Infrastructure to the user
- provision of Integrating Infrastructure dependent help (more task and context specific than the basic help function)
- check user inputs and send the correct information to the other services
- management of a system wide user directory
- system wide messaging between users

The last two functions could be seen as basic functions in a distributed system. But since the HF uses the specific functionality of the other services of the Integrating Infrastructure they are included here.

7.4.8.2.7 HF Functions related to application programs

The HF must provide the means to realize the interaction between the human user and any used application programs.

The necessary functionality to do so is included here.
Typical functions of this group are:

- presentation of the functionality of the application
  programs to the user in a way that the user can
  understand it by using information from the application
  interface model.
- monitoring of the status of the application program to
  the user
- provision of application dependent help
- check user inputs and send the correct information to
  the application programs

7.4.8.3 Overview of Protocols and Layered Services

Figure 7-17 shows an overview of the protocols which are
used and provided by the HF and the layered services used.

For the communication with the rest of the IIS the HF
provides an access protocol and uses the access protocols of
the other services of the IIS.

For the communication between different entities of the HF
an HF-agent protocol is used.

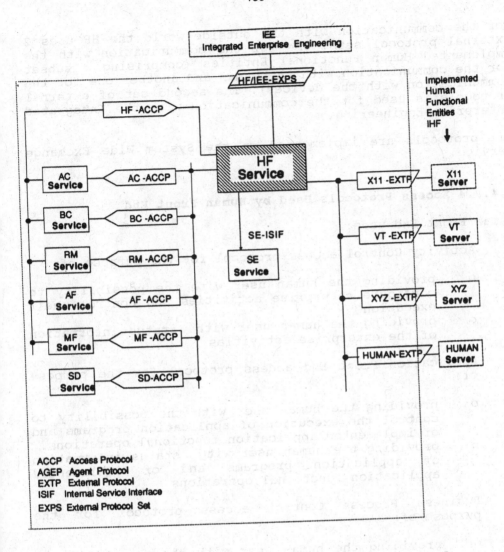

Figure 7-17: Protocols and Layered Services used and provided by the Human Front End

For the communication with the outside world the HF uses 2 external protocol sets. One for the communication with the implemented Human Functional Entities (comprising a subset for the communication with the human and another one for the communication with the devices). The second set of external protocols is used for the communication with the Integrated Enterprise Engineering.

All protocols are implemented on the System Wide Exchange Service.

7.4.8.4 Access Protocols Used by Human Front End

Human Front End uses:

- Activity Control access protocol for the purpose of:

  o providing the human user with the possibility to configure enterprise activities and control their execution
  o providing the human user with status information of the enterprise activities

- Application Front End access protocol for the purpose of:

  o providing the human user with the possibility to control the execution of application programs and of implemented application functional operations.
  o providing the human user with status information of application programs and of implemented application functional operations

- Business Process Control access protocol for the purpose of:

  o providing the human user with the possibility to configure business processes and control their execution
  o providing the human user with status information of the business processes

- Machine Front End access protocol for the purpose of:

  o providing the human user with the possibility to control machine resources and implemented machine functional operations
  o providing the human user with status information of the machines and implemented machine functional operations

- Resource Management access protocol for the purpose of:

  o providing the user with information about available resources and with the possibility to influence the disposition of resources
  o providing the human user with status information of resources

- System Wide Data access protocol for the purpose of:

  o Storage and retrieval of data

7.4.8.5 Access Protocol of Human Front End

The Human Front End access protocol is provided to internal clients for the purpose of :

- allowing clients to deliver data to the human user present information (including status information), alarm messages etc.
- allowing clients to request data or action from a human user
  request for user input, request for human functional operation status information, human resource status information
- management of human resources, control implemented human functional operations

7.4.8.6 Agent Protocol of Human Front End

Human Front End entities communicate through the HF agent protocol for the purpose of

- locating human users system wide
- messaging between human users
- connecting the user-corresponding HF entity to a client of the integrating infrastructure (subcontracting of different HF entities on different nodes)

7.4.8.7 External Protocols of Human Front End

7.4.8.7.1 External Protocol between Human Front End and Implemented Human Functional Entities

As a front end of the Integrating Infrastructure the Human Front End Service contains not only a protocols with the other services of the Integrating Infrastructure but also external protocols to the outside world.

One external protocol set specifies the communication between the Human Front End and the Implemented Human Functional Entities.

Compared with the other front ends this external protocol contains two parts. The first one is the protocol with the external devices used (e.g. crt terminal with control software and device agent) and the second part which is implemented on top of the first one is the protocol with the human user himself.

The first protocol is quite similar to the external protocols of the other front ends and allows to

- present (output) information in the defined way on the external devices using the capabilities of the special device
- get information from the external device

The second protocol defines the interaction between user and system (HF) and provides the means

- for the human to use the basic HF functions for e.g.:

  start-up, text editing, graphics editing (drawing), user messaging, undo/redo, help, presentation configuration, interaction configuration, etc.

- for the interaction between the user and the other Integrating Infrastructure services (via HF), e.g.:

  help, requirement and presentation of status information, data storage and retrieval, management and control of machine resources and machine functional entities, configuration and control of business processes and enterprise activities, monitoring and control of resource management, etc.

- for the interaction between the user and application programs e.g.:

  control the execution of an application program, get information from an application program, application dependent help etc.

7.4.8.7.2 External Protocol between Human Front End and Integrated Enterprise Engineering

The HF uses this external protocol to communicate with the Integrated Enterprise Engineering for the following purposes.

- control the insertion and withdrawing of releases of

  o application interface models in operation
  o interaction models in operation
  o user models in operation
  o device models in operation

7.4.8.8 Layered Services Provided by Human Front End

7.4.8.9 Layered Services Used by Human Front End

The Human Front End uses the Services of the System Wide Exchange to implement its access protocol, its agent protocol and its external protocols.

7.4.9 The Application Front End Service

Application Programs of today contain both the specifics of the data processing as well as the business environments. Data accesses, data communications, data presentation, business rules and business processes are coded into the application programs. Application programs containing all these specifics are therefore not very flexible and their portability is very restricted.

Furthermore any change in these environments results in a change in the application program, which contributes to the considerable maintenance load of today.

The CIM-OSA Integrating Infrastructure provides a set of specified services, which will **isolate** the application programs from the specifics of the business and data processing environments.

7.4.9.1 Purpose

The purpose of the Application Front End Service is to provide a defined set of services for the interaction between the application programs and the services of the CIM-OSA Integrating Infrastructure with the following objectives :

- provide a higher level of stability to the application programs.
- promote the building of portable application programs.
- facilitate the building of compatible application components, which work together as one system.

- Provide the **same mode of interaction** between the CIM-OSA Integrating Infrastructure and the Implemented Application Functional Entities by :

  o Allowing all application programs to interact with the services of the CIM-OSA Integrating Infrastructure via a single protocol, the Application Front End Service - External Protocol thereby allowing the application programs to consider the entire CIM-OSA Integrating Infrastructure as a single functional entity, hiding the internal structure.

  This protocol is independent of the business and data processing environments, and therefore these environments are no longer a restriction to the portability and a source of maintenance of application programs.

  o providing a service to any of the CIM-OSA Integrating Infrastructure Services for the execution of an application program. For this purpose the Application Front End Service offers a set of services via the Application Front End Service - Access Protocol , to start, interrupt, restart and terminate application programs. The services of the CIM-OSA Integrating Infrastructure therefore do not need to interact with the different application programs.

7.4.9.2 Functions Within Application Front

The functions are logically categorised as follows :

7.4.9.2.1 Application Front End Set-Up Functional Units

These functions facilitate the set up of an implemented application functional entity so that an application program is ready to be executed.

The functions will

- arrange that a program, which should be activated and is available as source code, will be compiled.
- arrange that a program, which should be activated and is available object code, will be loaded.
- arrange that an instance of a program, which is loaded is activated for execution. Thereby all necessary components, such as coprocessor and storage, are also activated for execution of that instance of the program.

- ensure that private application owned by services of the CIM-OSA Integrating Infrastructure can only be activated by the service that owns the private application program.

7.4.9.2.2 Application Front End Control Functional Unit

Contains a set of functions required to control the execution of an application program by the implemented application functional entity.

These functions will

- start the execution of an instance of an activated program and pass the run time parameters and data to that activated instance of the program.
- interrupt the execution of an instance of an activated program
- restart the execution of an interrupted instance of an activated program
- terminate the execution of an instance of an activated program. This means the program may come to an uncontrolled end.
- verify the schema of the available data and the schema required by the application program. If the application program required a different schema, schema conversion will be requested from the System Wide Data Service. The Application Front End Service does not provide schema conversion.
- monitor the execution of an application program.

7.4.9.2.3 Application Front End External Request Function Unit

These functions allow the application programs to use the services of the CIM-OSA Integrating Infrastructure, and to interact with other application programs.

These functions will handle requests

- for data storage and retrieval from the application programs. For this purpose the System Wide Data Service will be used
- for data input and output from and to humans. For this purpose the Human Front End Service will be used
- for data input and output from and to machines. For this purpose the Machine Front End Service will be used.
- for data exchange between two activated instances of application programs. This facilitates the interaction between to application programs.
- from application programs to start, interrupt, restart, terminate and abort application programs.

- from application programs to send or receive messages and data from external entities (e.g. an application program send data to a suppliers). For this purpose the System Wide Exchange Services will be used.

7.4.9.2.4 Application Front End Status Reporting Functional Unit

These functions allow the CIM-OSA Integrating Infrastructure to react to unsolicited status reports and will handle all:

- status information received from application programs and it distribute this status information to the relevant service of the CIM-OSA Integrating Infrastructure
- unsolicited status information received from application programs and it distribute this information to the Activity Control Service and/or the Human Front End Service.
- unsolicited status information received from private application programs and it distribute this unsolicited status information to the service which is the owner of the private application program.

7.4.9.2.5 Application Front End Build Time Functional Unit

These functions provide the specific support for the build time environment and will control the execution of:

- programs of the CIM-OSA Integrated Enterprise Engineering
- application programs for test purposes in the build time environment
- application programs for test purposes in the run time environment, whenever testing of a combination of new and existing components and the existing components are only available in the run time environment.

7.4.9.3 Overview of the Protocols of the Application Front End Service

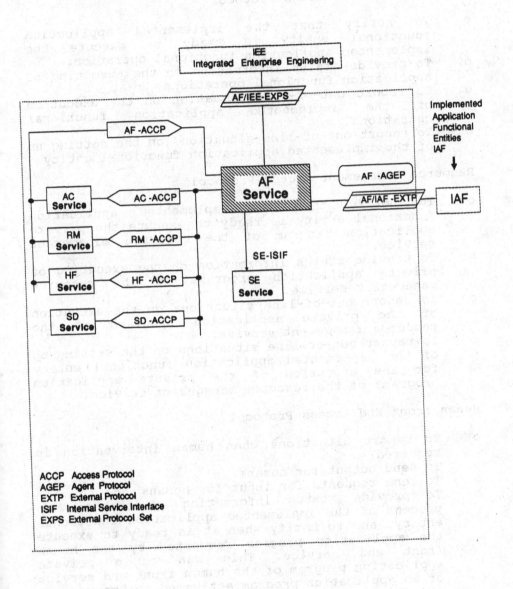

ACCP Access Protocol
AGEP Agent Protocol
EXTP External Protocol
ISIF Internal Service Interface
EXPS External Protocol Set

Figure 7-18: Protocols and Layered Services used and provided by the Application Front End

7.4.9.4 Access Protocols Used by Application Front End

The Application Front End Service uses the following protocols:

- Activity Control Access Protocol

  o To notify that the implemented application functional entity is ready to execute the implemented application functional operation.
  o To provide status information on the executing of application functional operations.
  o To report out-of-line situation on the execution of the implemented application functional operations.
  o To report out-of-line situations on the setting up of the implemented application functional entity.

- Resource Management Access Protocol

  o To notify that the implemented application functional entity is ready to execute the private application program of the resource management service.
  o To provide status information on the executing of private application programs of the resource management service.
  o To report out-of-line situations on the execution of the private application programs of the resource management service.
  o To report out-of-line situations on the setting up of the implemented application functional entity for the execution of the private application programs of the resource management service.

- Human Front End Access Protocol

  o To report situations when human intervention is required
  o To send output for humans
  o To send requests for input for humans
  o To provide status information of the set up process of the implemented application functional entity, and to notify when it is ready to execute the application program requested by the human front end service. This can be a private application program of the human front end service or an application program activated on the request of a human.
  o To report out-of-line situations on the setting up of the implemented application functional entity.
  o To provide status information on the execution of the above-mentioned application programs to the human front end service.

o   To report out-of-line situations on the execution
      of the above-mentioned application programs to the
      human front end service.

-    System Wide Data Access Protocol

o   To retrieve data requested by application programs
o   To store data output from application programs
o   To request schema conversions
o   To update and retrieve the state variables
      necessary to rum the implemented application
      functional operations.

7.4.9.5 Access Protocols of Application Front End

The Application Front End Service provides its access
protocol to its clients for the following purposes:

-    To set up the implemented application functional
     entity.
-    To control the execution of implemented application
     functional operations.
-    To control the execution of application programs of
     users or private application programs.
-    To obtain status information on the setting up of
     implemented application functional entities.
-    To obtain status information on the execution of
     implemented application functional operations,
     application programs of users and private application
     programs.
-    To test the execution of implemented application
     functional operations, in the build time environment
     and in a combination of build time and run time
     environment.

7.4.9.6 Agent Protocols Used by Application Front End

Application Front End entities communicate through the
Application Front End Agent Protocol for the following
purposes:

-    To subcontract implemented application functional
     entities.
-    To transfer data from one application to another.
-    To request activation of an application program.
-    To request the start, interrupt, restart, termination
     or abortion of an application program.
-    To query the status of a subcontract.
-    To query the status of the set up of an implemented
     application functional entity.
-    To query the status of the execution of an implemented
     application functional operation or an application
     program.

7.4.9.7 External Protocols Used by Application Front End

Application Programs interact with the CIM-OSA Integrating Infrastructure through the external protocol of the Application Front End Service, for the following purposes:

- to allow the application programs to exchange information.
- To allow the application programs to store and retrieve data.
- To allow application programs to interact with other application programs, irrespective of the node on which they run.
- To allow application programs to feed back status information and out-of-line situations (exception conditions).

7.4.9.8 Layered Services Provided by Application Front End Service

7.4.9.9 Layered Services Used by Application Front End Service

The Application Front End Service uses the System Wide Exchange Service to implement its access protocols, its agent protocols and its external protocols.

7.4.10 The Business Process Control (BC) Service

7.4.10.1 Purpose

The purpose of the Business Process Control Service is to provide the services to control the (possibly distributed) Business Processes with the following objectives :

1. Isolate the application systems from the organisational environment.
2. Provide a defined set of CIM-OSA services for Business Processes
3. Provide a higher level of stability to the application systems which actually support the enterprise activities.
4. Facilitate the building of compatible application components, which can work together as one system.
5. Promote the portability of applications.

Business Process Control provides the following services :

- to manage the execution of Business Processes,
- to control the sequencing and synchronization of Enterprise Activities by invoking the rules specifying the flow of action (procedural and operational rule sets),
- to transfer the control of a part or all of a Business Process from one CIM-OSA node to another CIM-OSA node,
- to control the release of new configurations of Business Processes, and applies the changes to the relevant occurrences of the reconfigured Business Process. It will not apply any changes to executing Enterprise Activities, and
- to allow for comprehensive system-user visibility and control over Business Processes.

7.4.10.2 Functions Within Business Process Control

The functions are logically categorized into Functional Units :

7.4.10.2.1 Business Process Control - Execution Control Functional Unit

contains a set of functions allowing a Business Process to be started, controlled, interrupted and stopped which will:

- provide to the user the possibility to take the initiative of creating a Business Process Occurrence.
- set up and activate a scheduled occurrence of the Business Process.
  The first Enterprise Activity will be started according to the Business Rules by issuing a "Start Enterprise Activity Occurrence" to Activity Control.
- interrupt the execution of a Business Process Occurrence.
- terminate the execution of an Occurrence of the Business Process after the completion of the primitive being executed. this is a controlled end.
- abort the execution of an Occurrence of the Business Process immediately, This is an uncontrolled end.
- restart the execution of a Business Process Occurrence suspended by an "Interrupt Business Process Occurrence" function.
- process the Procedural Rule Set of the Business Processes Occurrence.
- process the Operational Rule Set of the Business Processes to support the mode of operation.

7.4.10.2.2 Business Processes Control - Scheduling Functional Unit

contains a set of functions related to the scheduling of Business Processes.

These functions will :

-   handle requests to schedule an existing Business Process Occurrence. After the scheduling, the Schedule Status becomes "scheduled".
-   handle requests to deschedule an existing scheduled Business Process Occurrence. After this descheduling, the occurrence still exists but has Schedule Status "descheduled". It will only be removed from this "descheduled" status by a request issued by the Human Front End.
-   handle requests to make a new schedule for an already scheduled Business Process Occurrence.
-   process a new unsolicited schedule for a Business Process Occurrence from Resource Management.
-   process a new unsolicited Schedule Status for a Business Process Occurrence.
-   react to reports that the scheduling window was moved. As a result, new occurrences can be created for the newly "opened" time period.
-   change the priority of one, or a defined set, or all Occurrences of a given Business Process.

7.4.10.2.3 Business Process Control - Change Control Functional Unit

contains a set of functions allowing to change a Business Process which will:

-   Process the release of a new Business Process configuration which is released for use.
-   process the release of a Business Process reconfiguration which is an updated version of an existing Business Process, and
-   provide the possibility to reconfigure one particular Occurrence of a Business Process. Only this particular Occurrence is changed, not the Released Implemented Requirements Definition Model. There are constraints imposed to this function.

7.4.10.2.4 Business Process Control - Status Reporting Functional Unit

contains a set of functions related to status reporting which will provide :

- the possibility of passing unsolicited status information to Business Process Control. Business Process Control will analyze this status information and, if necessary, react or initiate appropriate action depending on the analysis.
- the status of a Business Process Occurrence to the Service activating these functions. These functions handle the Execution Status and the Schedule Status.
- the possibility of passing unsolicited status information related to a resource to Business Process Control. Business Process Control will analyze this status information and, if necessary, react or initiate appropriate action depending on the analysis.

7.4.10.2.5 Business Process Control - Distributed Control Functional Unit

contains a set of functions related to the distributed execution of a Business Process.

These functions will :

- transfer the execution of a Business Process Occurrence to the Business Process Control of the other node.
- subcontract the control of the execution of an Occurrence of a lower lever Business Process to the Business Process Control of the other node.
- subcontract the control of the execution of a set of Enterprise Activity Occurrences belonging to a Business Process to the Business Process Control of the other node.
- provide the possibility of retransferring the control of the execution of a set of Enterprise Activity Occurrences or a lower level Business Process Occurrence to the Business Process Control of the original node.
- provide the Business Process Control of the node to which control was subcontracted the possibility of passing unsolicited status information to the Business Process Control of the original node. Business Process Control will analyze this status information and, if necessary, react or initiate appropriate action depending on the analysis.

7.4.10.3 Overview of Protocols and Layered Services

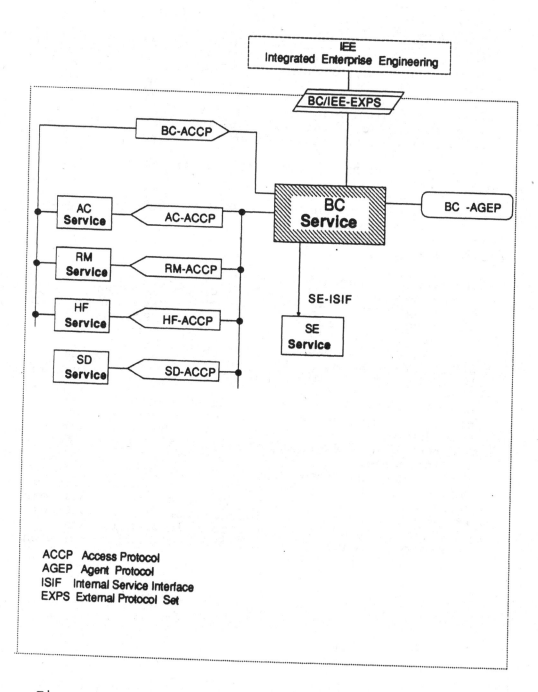

Figure 7-19: Protocols and Layered Services used and
provided by the Business Process Control

7.4.10.4 Access Protocols Used by Business Process Control

Business Process Control uses the following access protocols:

- System Wide Data Access Protocol: to obtain the descriptions of Business Processes (models and occurrences) to control their execution (e.g. input/output request, status on input/output request).
- Resource Management Access Protocol: to schedule Business Processes with or without resource reservation.
- Human Front End Access Protocol: for reporting out of line situations of Business Process to Human Front End.
- Activity Control Access Protocol: to control the execution of Enterprise Activities by Activity Control.

7.4.10.5 Access Protocol of Business Process Control

Business Process Control provides the Business Process Control Access Protocol to its clients for the following purposes:

- to schedule Business Processes,
- to provide status information on Business Processes,
- to manage the execution of Business Processes,
- to update models and occurrences of Business Processes, and
- to report out of line situations from the executed Enterprise Activities.

7.4.10.6 Agent Protocol of Business Process Control

Business Process Control entities communicate through the Business Process Control agent protocol for the following purpose:

to manage the transfer and the subcontracting of control between Business Process Control Services on different CIM-OSA nodes.

7.4.10.7 External Protocol of Business Process Management

The CIM-OSA Integrated Enterprise Engineering communicates with Business Process Control through the Business Process Control External Protocol for the following purposes:

- release of new Business Processes,
- release of new editions of existing Business Processes,
- withdrawing of existing Business Processes.

7.4.10.8 Layered Services Provided by Business Process Control

7.4.10.9 Layered Services Used by Business Process Control

The Business Process Control Service uses the services of the System Wide Data Service to implement its access protocols and its agent protocols.

7.4.11 The Activity Control (AC) Service

7.4.11.1 Purpose

The purpose of the Activity Control Service is to provide a defined set of services to control, monitor and service the (possibly distributed) Enterprise Activities with the following objectives :

1. isolate the application systems from the Data Processing environment,
2. isolate the application systems from the Data Processing environment,
3. provide a higher level of stability to the applications systems which support the enterprise activities,
4. facilitate the building of compatible application components which can work together as one system,
5. promote the portability of application programs,
6. provide **the same** control functions for the execution of Implemented Functional Operations by a human, a machine or an application program,
7. interact with the Resource Management service to monitor and control the execution of Implemented Functional Operations,
8. provide basic support for the synchronization of Implemented Functional Operations,
9. provide full status information on the progress of Enterprise Activities and Implemented Functional Operations.

The Activity Control Service provides the following services:

- to provide status information on Enterprise Activities,
- to manage the execution of Enterprise Activities,
- to update models and occurrences of Enterprise Activities,
- to report out of line situations from the executing Front Ends, and

- to manage transfer of control between Activity Control Services on different CIM-OSA nodes for distributed Enterprise Activities.

7.4.11.2 Functions Within Activity Control

7.4.11.2.1 Activity Control - Execution Control Functional Unit

a set of functions allowing an Enterprise Activity to be started, to be interrupted and to be stopped.

These functions will :

- create, set up and activate an Occurrence of the Enterprise Activity
- interrupt the execution of an Enterprise Activity Occurrence.
- terminate the execution of an Occurrence of the Enterprise Activity after the completion of the primitive being executed. This is a controlled end.
- abort the execution of an Occurrence of the Enterprise Activity immediately. This is an uncontrolled end.
- restart the execution of an Occurrence of the Enterprise Activity suspended by an "Interrupt Enterprise Activity" function. Depending on a parameter, the execution is resumed at the point of interruption or restarted at the beginning of the interrupted Implemented Functional Operation.

7.4.11.2.2 Activity Control - Change Control Functional Unit

a set of functions allowing to change the occurrences of constructs of the enterprise activities which will :

- provide the possibility to reconfigure one particular Occurrence of an Enterprise Activity. Only this particular Occurrence is changed, not the Released Implemented Requirements Definition Model. (There are constraints imposed on this.)
- provide the possibility to reconfigure an Implemented Functional Operation in one particular Occurrence of an Enterprise Activity. Only the Implemented Functional Operation of the particular Occurrence is changed, not the Released Implemented Requirements Definition Model.
- process the release of a new Enterprise Activity, configured in the Particular Requirements Definition Model.
- process the release of an updated version of an existing Enterprise Activity, reconfigured in the Particular Requirements Definition Model.
- provide for the release for use of uploaded programs from the Machine Front End.

- handle change Events on all Occurrences of an Enterprise Activity that has been modified in the Particular Requirements Definition Model and released for use.

7.4.11.2.3 Activity Control - Status Reporting Functional Unit

a set of functions related to status reporting which will :

- provide the Front End Services the possibility of passing unsolicited status information to Activity Control. Activity Control will analyze this status information and, if necessary, react or initiate appropriate action depending on the analysis.
- provide the Resource Management the possibility of passing unsolicited status information to Activity Control. Activity Control will analyze this status information and, if necessary, react or initiate appropriate action depending on the analysis.
- provide the services of the CIM-OSA IIS the possibility to query the Execution Status of an Occurrence of an Enterprise Activity.
- provide the services of the CIM-OSA IIS the possibility to query Status of an Implemented Functional Operation in an Enterprise Activity Occurrence.

7.4.11.2.4 Activity Control - Distributed Control Functional Unit

a set of functions related to the distributed execution of a Enterprise Activities which will:

- transfer control of the execution of an Enterprise Activity Occurrence.
- transfer control of an Implemented Application Functional Operation.
- transfer the control of the execution of an Implemented Application Functional Operation of an Enterprise Activity Occurrence to the Activity Control of the other node, if the execution is not yet completed.
- handle the request for transferring the control of the execution of an Implemented Application Functional Operation of an Enterprise Activity or a complete Enterprise Activity to the Activity Control of an other node.

7.4.11.3 Overview of Protocols and Layered Services

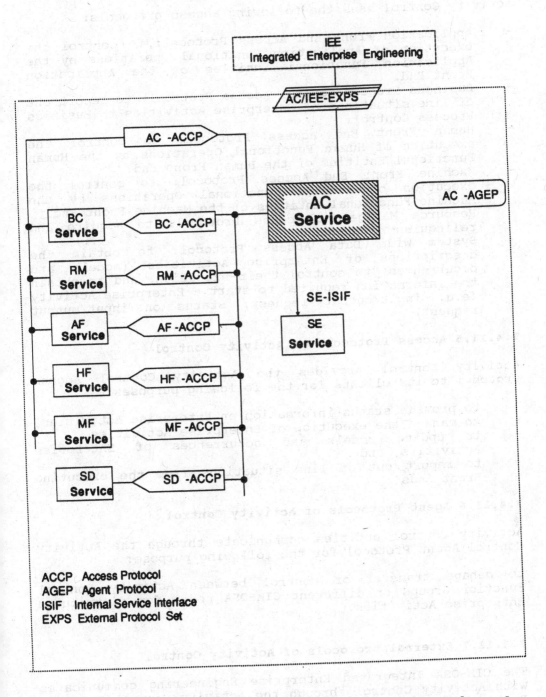

ACCP   Access Protocol
AGEP   Agent Protocol
ISIF   Internal Service Interface
EXPS   External Protocol Set

Figure 7-20: Protocols and Layered Services used and
Provided by the Activity Control

7.4.11.4 Access Protocols Used by Activity Control

Activity Control uses the following access protocols:

- Application Front End Access Protocol: to control the execution of Application Functional Operations by the Application Functional Entities of the Application Front End.
- Business Process Control Access Protocol: to report out of line situations of Enterprise Activities to Business Process Control.
- Human Front End Access Protocol: to control the execution of Human Functional Operations by the Human Functional Entities of the Human Front End.
- Machine Front End Access Protocol: to control the execution of Machine Functional Operations by the Machine Functional Entities of the Machine Front End.
- Resource Management Access Protocol: to acquire and relinquish resources
- System Wide Data Access Protocol: to obtain the descriptions of Enterprise Activities (models and occurrences) to control their execution, and to obtain the information required to start a Enterprise Activity (e.g. input/output request, status on input/output request).

7.4.11.5 Access Protocols of Activity Control

Activity Control provides the Activity Control Access Protocol to its clients for the following purposes:

- to provide status information on Enterprise Activities,
- to manage the execution of Enterprise Activities,
- to update models and occurrences of Enterprise Activities, and
- to report out of line situations from the executing Front Ends.

7.4.11.6 Agent Protocols of Activity Control

Activity Control entities communicate through the Activity Control Agent Protocol for the following purpose:

to manage transfer of control between Activity Control Function Groups on different CIM-OSA nodes for distributed Enterprise Activities.

7.4.11.7 External protocols of Activity Control

The CIM-OSA Integrated Enterprise Engineering communicates with Activity Control through the Activity Control External Protocol for the following purposes :

- release of new Enterprise Activities,
- release of new editions of existing Enterprise Activities,
- withdrawing of existing Enterprise Activities.

7.4.11.8 Layered Services Provided by Activity Control

7.4.11.9 Layered Services Used by Activity Control

The Activity Control Service uses the services of the System Wide Exchange Service to implement its access protocol and its agent protocol.

7.4.12 The Resource Management (RM) Service

7.4.12.1 Purpose

Resource Management is a distributed service which has the purpose of overall, system-wide, management of the enterprise resources as required for the proper execution of Business Process occurrences and their constituent Enterprise Activities. Such management may be achieved in either a centralized or distributed manner (according to user choice), by assigning responsibility for given (sub)sets of resources to specified Resource Management services.

In performing its tasks, Resource Management is designed to achieve the following:

1. Isolation of the applications from environmental concerns of resource management, thereby reducing Application complexity and maintenance workload, and promoting portability of Applications;
2. Provision of common, high level, resource management facilities to both Activity Control and Business Process Control;
3. Facilitation of Business Process/Enterprise Activity occurrence scheduling according to dynamic operational constraints (resource availability);
4. Provision of adequate functional support for configurable, user-defined, resource management/optimisation algorithms at various levels of sophistication; and
5. Allowing for comprehensive system-user visibility and control over resource management.

7.4.12.2 Functions Within Resource Management

the functions performed within Resource Management in order to provide its service are categorized here into a number of Functional Units :

7.4.12.2.1 Resource Management - Acquisition Functional Unit

These functions will :

- attempt an immediate acquisition of a resource for an Occurrence of a Business Process, Enterprise Activity, or Implemented Functional Operation.
- according to a parameter supplied, cause a specified instance, or all instances of a given type of resource in one or more polls, to be
  o marked temporarily unavailable for subsequent reservation or acquisition (blocked), or
  o returned to the pool (i.e. unblocked after a previous blocking).

7.4.12.2.2 Resource Management - Reservation Functional Unit

These functions will :

- attempt to reserve a resource for an occurrence of a Business Process, Enterprise Activity, or Implemented Functional Operation.
  All resource reservation requests specify the time from which they are to be reserved, and an estimate of the period from then on for which they will need to be assigned.
- reallocate a reserved resource by firstly relinquishing a previous resource reservation, and then to reserving or acquiring it for a different occurrence of a Business Process, Enterprise Activity, or Implemented Functional Operation.

7.4.12.2.3 Resource Management - Relinquishement Functional Unit

These functions :

- return an assigned or reserve resource to a resource pool.
- record the feed-back of resource consumption made during the assignment of the resource.

7.4.12.2.4 Resource Management - Scheduling Functional Unit

These functions will :

- schedule a single Business Process occurrence. The schedule is calculated based upon current expectations of resource availabilities, inserted into the appropriate Business Process occurrence description, and the Business Process occurrence is marked as "scheduled". Reservations are made depending on the conforming group active at the time of association to Resource Management's client.
- reschedule a single Business Process occurrence, and depending on the active conforming group, make resource reservations where needed and relinquish any "old" reservations, or to
- perform "what-if" simulations of the consequences of rescheduling a single Business Process occurrence according to supplied parameters.
- change the length of the scheduling window. If the length is decreased, no further action is taken (i.e. current resource commitment beyond the new window are honoured). However, if the window is lengthened resource commitments are made for the newly "opened" time period.
- deschedule a Business Process occurrence. If this scheduling releases resources which can then be used to bring forward other Business Process occurrences which are scheduled later than the desired times, the current window is re-optimised.
- recalculate the scheduling of Business Process occurrences for the current scheduling window, and reoptimise the allocations for the current window when the current resource allocations are found to be unsuitable.
  As a result of the rescheduling, a number of reserved resources may be withdraw and some Business Process occurrences rescheduled or descheduled.

7.4.12.2.5 Resource Management - Status Monitoring Functional Unit

These functions will :

- read and return the Resource Status and Resource Blocking Status to the request originator. They can fulfil the request for either a defined instance of resource type, all instances of a given type in one or more pools, or for all resources in one or more pools.
- indicate, among other conditions, a failure of a resource (making it unusable), or when a failed resource becomes usable again.

- will change the resource status accordingly, and if it is currently reserved or assigned, the using BP/EA/IFO is either

  o   interrupted, or

  o   terminated, and the resource is relinquished.
- modify one or more Resource Management Thresholds.
- maintain the Resource Status and Resource Blocking Status.
- maintain the "reporting counts" for all resource. Whenever a reporting count is changed such that a given threshold is exceeded, an "alarm state" is entered. On entering an alarm state generate an alarm message to a defined responsible user.
- periodically check the condition of all reserved resources. If it is found that a reserved resource has not been assigned at the expected schedule, an attempt will be made to estimate the likely delay by issuing an inquiry to the client who reserved the resource. If the estimated delay results in other Business Process occurrences being delayed beyond a certain threshold, the necessary rescheduling will be performed; and
- periodically move the current scheduling window, and triggers the scheduling process to determine resource requirements/reservations for the newly "opened" period. If any new Business Process Control will be prompted to re-scan its occurrence database.

7.4.12.2.6 Resource Management - Configuration Control Functional Unit

These functions will :

- modify the resource database to reflect a change in the capacity of a given (already defined) resource type in a given pool.
- replace the currently active version of the resource database with another.
- modify the definition of a defined resource i.e. change recorded properties of the resource.
- add a new resource type and definition to the currently active version of the resource database.
- remove an existing resource type/definition from the currently active version of the resource database.

7.4.12.2.7 Resource Management - Subcontract Functional Unit

These functions will :

- subcontract a set of requests to a peer, the results of which are to be returned to the calling RM.
- re-route a received request to an established subcontractor.

-   receive and handle reports from a Resource Management subcontractor to report progress. If the report indicates final completion of the requested subcontract, the subcontract is terminated.

7.4.12.2.8 Resource Management - Internal Functional Unit

These functions, which are used by the Resource Management Service internally, will :

-   monitor all pending requests and filter all incoming and outgoing PDUs/SDUs, keeping a log of which requests are outstanding at any given time; and periodically scans this log to attempt to determine whether a generated request has been "lost". If this occurs, internally generate a PDU/SDU indicating non-response to a request, and distributes it to the original requestor.
-   provide the Resource Management the possibility to perform user supplied resource optimisation algorithms as private application programs of RMP through the Application Front End Service in the form of Application Functional Operations.
-   include mechanisms for registration, starting and terminating of the private AFO's.

7.4.12.3 Overview of Protocols and Layered Services

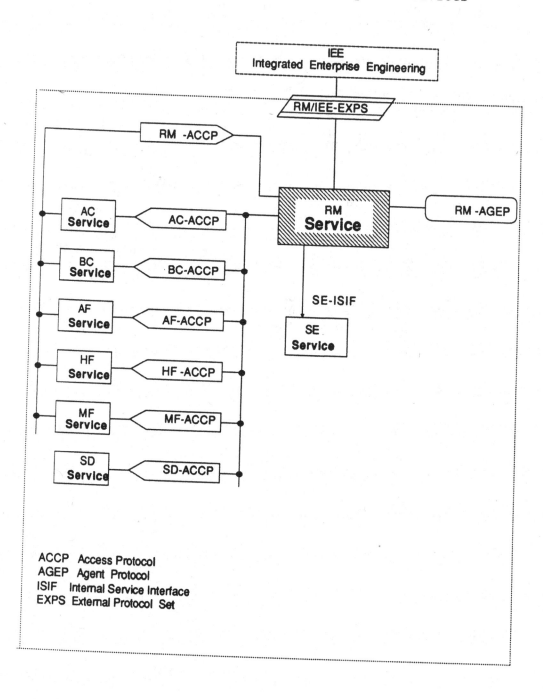

Figure 7-21: Protocols and Layered Services used and provided by the Resource Management

7.4.12.4 Access Protocols Used by Resource Management

Resource Management uses:

- the **Activity Control** access protocol for reporting out of line situations concerning resources, and to request status information;
- the **Application Front End** access protocol to start and stop a Private Application Functional Operation;
- the **Business Process Control** access protocol for the scheduling of Business Processes and to request status information on Business Processes;
- the **Human Front End** access protocol to control and monitor human resources;
- the **Machine Front End** access protocol to control and monitor human resources; and
- the **System Wide Data** access protocol to obtain the descriptions of the resources managed by Resource Management (e.g. input/output request, status on input/output request).

7.4.12.5 Access Protocol of Resource Management

Resource Management provides the Resource Management access protocol to its clients for the following purposes:

- to manage the resources,
- to schedule Business Processes with or without resource reservation,
- to provide status information on resources, and
- to update configuration of resources.

7.4.12.6 Agent Protocol of Resource Management

Resource Management entities communicate through the Resource Management Agent Protocol for the purpose of managing the transfer of control between, and the issuing and monitoring of subcontracts to, Resource Management peers.

7.4.12.7 External Protocols of Resource Management

Resource Management participates in an external protocol to the **Integrated** Enterprise Engineering (IEE) in order to support the orderly release of a new Resource Model.

7.4.12.8 Layered Services Provided by Resource Management

7.4.12.9 Layered Services Used by Resource Management

The Resource Management Service uses the services of the System Wide Data Service to implement its access protocol and its agent protocol.

7.4.13 IIS Relation to State of the Art

The most important papers and reports related to CIM Implementation Architectures have been analyzed and compared with the CIM-OSA IIS concepts:

- NBS AMRF: Automated Manufacturing Research Facility, in particular the IISS (Integrated Information Support System)
- ISO TC 184/SC5/WG1 N51: Ottawa Report on Reference Models for Manufacturing Standards.
- ANSI paper on Information Resource Dictionary System
- MAP, TOP and CNMA Specifications
- ISO TC97 and ISO/IEC JTC1/SC21: Open System Interconnection, including the emerging activities on Transaction Processing, Open Distributed Processing and Manufacturing Messaging Specifications, Remote Database Access,.
- DIN Technical Report 15: Many existing and emerging standards in the area of CIM like NC processing, Machine interfaces, graphic language and text/graphic interchange formats.

The analysis indicates that there are no similar activities which address the IIS services necessary to implement the Particular Implementation Description Models. This is especially true for the upper level services (BC, AC, RM) and partially for the Front Ends (MF, AF, HF, DM). Some generic concepts from ISO/IEC activities will be observed closely and adapted when appropriate.

7.4.14 Reference Architecture and Standardisation

Reference Models or architectures are a framework to build a set of coherent products. The effectiveness of such a framework depends on its acceptance by the market, i.e. the suppliers and users of the products. The risk of the investment in such products will be reduced considerably if the Reference Architecture becomes a standard.

Generally the standardisation is done in phases. The first phase is the standardisation of the Reference Model or Architecture. The second phase is the stepwise standardisation of the services and protocols which the specific products must conform.

The Figure 7-22 below illustrates this three fold, namely:

- In a generic way,
- An example from OSI, and
- A possible example for CIM-OSA.

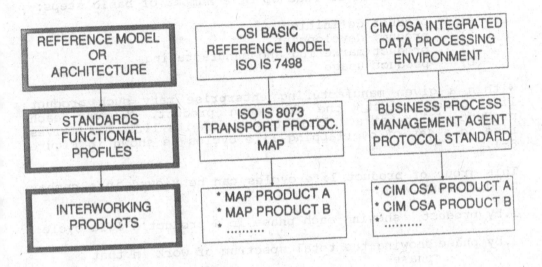

Figure 7-22: Standardisation of Reference Architectures

As can be seen from Figure 7-22, the first step towards the standardisation of CIM-OSA is to standardise the Reference Architecture, or a part thereof. This task was initiated in the first half of 1989 by the submission of a proposal to ISO TC184/SC5/WG1.

In the second phase the stepwise standardisation of the services and the protocols of the CIM-OSA Integrating Infrastructure can follow as the specifications evolve.

8. CIM-OSA System Life Cycle

8.1 Product Life Cycles

Product Life Cycles have been defined as a valuable concept to structure the different phases of the product life. Such a Product Life Cycle is made up of a number of basic steps:-

- A) product definition
- B) product development
- C) product marketing and manufacturing
- D) product usage

Within a given manufacturing enterprise many such product life cycles exist, one for each product. However each product will be at a different stage in its life. This gives rise to a set of overlapping life cycles as shown in Figure 8-1.

This group of product life cycles can be viewed in a number of different ways:-

1. by product showing each phase in a product's life cycle

2. by phase showing the total spectrum of work in that phase

3. by time showing a cross section of all the work within the enterprise at that instant of time

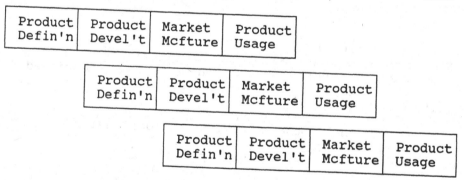

Figure 8-1: Overlapping Product Life Cycles

Not all phases may exist for all types of products (standard mass produced products cover all phases, one off made to order products may not need marketing phase).

In order that the tasks associated with each step of the Product Life Cycle may be executed in a controllable manner it will be necessary to define the procedures to be followed. These will take the form of company standards, work instructions, process sheets etc.

In CIM-OSA terms these will be the set of business processes, enterprise activities and procedural rules which totally describe the enterprise environment for each task within the Product Life Cycle. This is the CIM-OSA compliant enterprise system which is hosted by the CIM-OSA Integrating Infrastructure.

8.2 System Life Cycle

Whilst today's enterprise systems are in operation, their successors may be in the process of implementation. Strategic business plans under development today will set the stage for the systems implementations of tomorrow. Thus as an enterprise evolves over time the enterprise's systems will go through life cycles. We call the enterprise system life cycle the System Life Cycle. During this system life cycle the various business processes/enterprise activities describing the enterprise environment are designed.

In order that the various system design tasks may be executed in a controllable manner CIM-OSA has defined a system design environment - the Integrated Support Environment. This permits the enterprise environment for one task within the Product Life Cycle to be designed/updated independently from the environment for other tasks.

A single CIM sub-system within a particular enterprise may well be a standard product as far as the vendor of the basic sub-system is concerned but when customised to a particular enterprise it becomes a one off product as far as the particular enterprise is concerned. We need therefore to consider the life cycle for one off products (No product marketing required). In order to readily distinguish the phases of the System Life Cycle from those of the Product Life Cycle they are given different names:-

A)   System Requirements Specification
B)   System Design
C)   System Build and Release
D)   System Operation

The basic System Life Cycle for a business process is shown in Figure 8-2. Here it is seen that the creation and execution of a business process involves the following tasks:-

o   select an appropriate class of business process from a Partial Model o   particularise the selected business process by adding enterprise specific parameters to make an instance of the business process

o   release the Implementation Description Model, which contains the instance, into the operational system

o   add at execution time technical parameters and logistic variables to a copy of the released instance (an occurrence)

Each of the steps in the CIM System Life Cycle will be further defined in a Section 8.3 of this document.

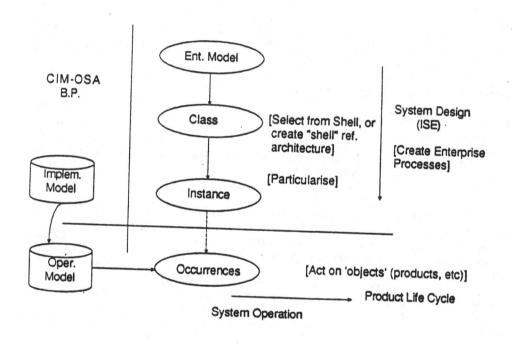

Figure 8-2: The Life Cycle of a Business Process

8.3 Relationships Between the Product and System Life Cycles

Whenever it is required to define a new or revised business process supporting part of the Product Life Cycle environment it will be necessary to carry out the tasks belonging to one or more phases of the System Life Cycle.

The different elements of the enterprise system may be developed independently. This means that several System Life Cycles will coexist. System Life Cycle tasks will be carried out under the control of CIM-OSA defined business processes of the Integrated Support Environment. These will guide the design/revision processes leading to creation of a new set of enterprise procedures associated with a new version of a Product Life Cycle. For example during the 'system build and release' phase of the System Life Cycle the business process etc. are released for use in controlling the tasks of the Product Life Cycle.

The relationship between the Product and System Life Cycles is summarized in Figure 8-3.

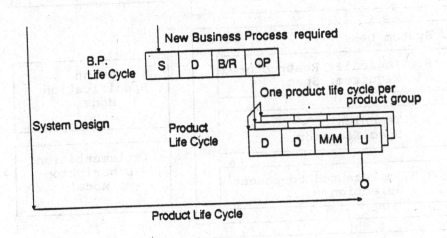

Figure 8-3: Relationships between the two Life Cycles

8.4 Contents of System Life Cycles

An overview of the System Life Cycle is given in the Figure 8-4. Although this diagram represents the System Life Cycle as a pure sequential phased process, iterations between adjacent phases are in practice necessary. Figure 8-4 relates the phases of the System Life Cycle to the Particular Models of CIM-OSA.

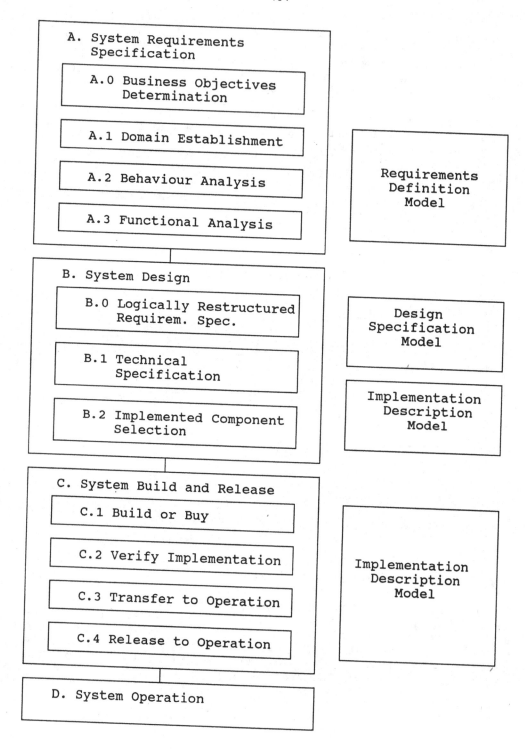

Figure "8-4: System Life Cycle

In the descriptions which follow, it should be noted that all the activities described within phases A, B and C (except for those parts which are specifically defined below as being unsupported by CIM-OSA) are all performed within the CIM-OSA Integrated Enterprise Engineering Environment (IEEE), whilst those of phase D are performed within the Integrated Enterprise Operational Environment (IEOE).

8.4.1 Phase A - System Requirements Specification

The first phase, "System Requirements Specification", is primarily concerned with the requirements definition, analysis and specification activities used to build a particularised CIM-OSA Requirements Definition Model. It addresses those parts of the enterprise to be modelled from each of the Function, Information Resource and Organisation Views of the Requirements Definition Model. This phase establishes a validated, integrated set of requirements for, constraints upon, and alternatives of implementation.

While some implementation concerns are inevitably addressed, it is the intention that these concerns are minimised as far as possible so as to concentrate attention on the real underlying needs of an enterprise in a manner minimally compromised by envisaged system realisations. Conversely, where it is desired that the requirements specification is to be formed in a way which is constrained by the current implementation, explicit constraints are introduced during this phase to control the subsequent ones appropriately.

Phase A is sub-divided into four parts:

o   A-0: Business Objectives Determination
o   A-1: Domain Establishment,
o   A-2: Behaviour Analysis, and
o   A-3: Functional Analysis.

These are described briefly below.

A-0: Business Objectives Determination

This is not directly supported by CIM-OSA, but is a prerequisite starting point for the System Life Cycle. Here, the enterprise's business objectives are determined for that part of the enterprise which is to be modelled and implemented according to CIM-OSA. The objectives are specified in terms of such things as markets, product groups and volumes, Return On Investment (ROI) and profit goals.

A-1: Domain Establishment

Given the determined objectives, this sub-phase is used to create a CIM-OSA description of the modelling 'domain' in terms of Business Process Events, Business Process Results, Declarative Rules, classes of required Business Processes, and classes of information.

The Business Process Events and Business Process Results identified serve to define the boundary interactions of the domain (i.e. its dynamic relation to any enclosing domains), while the declarative rules express (e.g. operational or cost) constraints imposed on the domain from outside. The classes of business processes are used to categorise the kind of tasks performed within the domain (e.g. 'design', 'produce' etc.), and the information classes serve to describe the main 'objects' of concern to the domain (e.g. product classes and their expected volumes).

In the first iteration of the life cycle for a given enterprise, the domain is the entire area of interest for modelling, while for subsequent iterations this sub-phase addresses organisational domains established during sub-phase A-2 (see below).

It is assumed that the Requirements Definition Model Organisational View will provide constructs for the expression of such domains.

A-2: Behaviour Analysis

Here, capacity and performance targets, cost constrains and organisational constraints, and so on, are used to further detail the identified classes of business processes, resulting in the creation of Procedural Rule Sets and an initial pool of Enterprise Activities to support the business processes.

Capacity/performance (and other kinds of) information are used in a broad manner to identify

o   lower level categorisations of business processes (e.g. a mass production process and a prototype production process) and classes of enterprise activities, and also to identify
o   lower level organisational domains and their objectives (for example, capacity requirements may indicate the need for two assembly plants).

For each new domain identified, a further iteration is performed via sub-phases A-1.

This phase (A-2) is reiterated sufficiently to break business processes of the current domain down to a level where all necessary classes of enterprise activities can be determined. At this stage, only the primary inputs and outputs of the activities are identified (the secondary and tertiary ones are the subject of sub-phase A-3), i.e. only the required functional capabilities are identified, not the methods used to realise the functions.

A-3: Functional Analysis

A-3 completes the specifications of the enterprise activities defined for the current domain.

For each of the enterprise activity categories an analysis is made to determine the alternative methods of function implementation which are possible (e.g. hole-making via either drilling, boring or cutting), and thereby to establish alternative, optional, sets of resources required and parameters needed to control the functions.

This results in the specification of alternative sets of secondary and tertiary inputs/outputs: from these complete enterprise activity descriptions, the set of external schemas to be supported by the Information Model are determined.

Each of these and all of the following phases are subject to verification employing simulation wherever possible.

8.4.2 Phase B - System Design

The purpose of Phase B, "System Design", is essentially to perform a quantitative analysis of the established Requirements Definition Model. Phase B is started by a restructuring of the requirement specifications taking into account the relevant enterprise constraints.

The resulting Design Specification Model is translated it into a form used for specifying the components (information and manufacturing technology) needed to implement the requirements.

This specification is expressed in the form of a Specified Implementation Description Model, consisting of:

o   Specified Function View,
o   Specified Information View
o   Specified Resource View (incl. specification of Specified Components), and
o   Specified Organisation View.

Phase B then concludes by selecting from available CIM-OSA compliant products a set of actual components which meet or exceed the requirements of the Specified Components. The final Build/Buy decisions (see description of sub-phase B-2 below) result in a model of the implemented enterprise system, now termed the Implementation Description Model, whose constituent parts are the

o   Implemented Functional View
o   Implemented Information View
o   Implemented Resource View (incl. specifications of Implemented Components), and
o   Implemented Organisation View.

Phase B is sub-divided into three main parts:

o   B-0: Logically restructured and optimised Requirement Specifications
o   B-1: Technical Specification, and
o   B-2: Implemented Component Selection.

These are described briefly below.

B-0: Logically restructured and optimised Requirement Specifications

to be defined

B-1: Technical Specification

Using the results of the Requirements Specification Phase, this sub-phase has the purpose of translating the requirements into quantitative descriptions of the required manufacturing and information technology components. Through material-flow (parts routing) and information-needs analysis, performance analysis, and so on, decisions are taken on such topics as:

o   actual means of implementing enterprise activities, through selection from available activity parameter sets, and determination of business process 'instance parameter' sets, functional operations, enterprise activity control structures;
o   volumes, physical location, performance, etc., of required resources (Specified Resource Model);
o   volumes, storage location, internal-schemas, etc., of required information;
o   responsibilities and authorisation for business processes, enterprise activities, resources, information, out-of-line situations, etc;
o   volumes, location, performance requirements, IDPE nodal configurations, etc., for functional components, functional operations; and
o   material flow models/material storage strategies and information models.
(NB: models have not been defined yet to express these dynamic 'flow' aspects).

B-2: Implemented Component Selection

Based upon the results of B-1, decisions are now taken by the enterprise on which physical CIM-OSA compliant components are to be used for implementation. Within established cost and other constraints, a decision may be taken to buy available CIM-OSA compliant components available on the market which meet or exceed the requirements of the Specified Components or, when not available, to build new ones.

The components subsequently selected are termed Implemented Components, and the (possibly altered) Specified Implementation Description Model becomes the Implementation Description Model.

8.4.3 Phase C - System Build and Release

Based upon the results and decisions of Phase B, Phase C "System Build and Release" is concerned with those activities necessary to bring the system into operation. This involves essentially the procuring (or building) of the necessary new or revised Implemented Components, integrating them into the existing system, and testing and releasing them for operation.

Phase C is sub-divided into four main parts:

o   C-1: Build or Buy and Integrate,
o   C-2: Verify Implementation,
o   C-3: Transfer to Operations, and
o   C-4: Release for Operations.

These are briefly described below.

C-1: Build or Buy and Integrate

This is where the enterprise purchases or builds the Implemented Components decided upon during sub-phase B-2, and physically integrates them into the existing system.

At the completion of this sub-phase the Implemented Components and underlying Implementation Description Model are said to be installed.

C-2: Verify Implementation

Here, the correct functioning of the installed Implemented Components, and the correctness of the underlying Implementation Description Model, are verified in a close-to-operational environment. It is expected that the IDPE's Integrating Infrastructure will, in support of this, provide a set of pseudo-operational facilities for the running of a

C-2: Verify Implementation

Here, the correct functioning of the installed Implemented Components, and the correctness of the underlying Implementation Description Model, are verified in a close-to-operational environment. It is expected that the IDPE's Integrating Infrastructure will, in support of this, provide a set of pseudo-operational facilities for the running of a test environment logically separated from, but physically integrated with, the current operational system.

At the completion of this sub-phase the Implemented Components and underlying Implementation Description Model are said to be verified.

C-3: Transfer to Operations

This sub-phase consists of such activities as operator training and customer acceptance testing, and making the verified Implemented Components and the underlying Implementation Description Model ready for release into operation. They are then said to be accepted.

C-4: Release for Operations

This consists of finally releasing the accepted Implemented Components and underlying Implementation Description Model for operation. The operational version of the accepted Implementation Description Model is released, from the Integrated Enterprise Engineering (IEE), for use by the Integrated Enterprise Operation (IEO). It is then termed the Released Implementation Description Model.

8.4.4 Phase D - System Operation

In this phase the released system is operated in order to effect the desired product life cycles, under operational control of the Integrating Infrastructure. This is accomplished via the creation, scheduling, and execution of parameterised instances of Business Processes derived from the underlying Released Implementation Description Model (but, here, also refer to the open issue stated later concerning the meaning of Business Processes/Procedural Rule Sets) in the Integrating Infrastructure.

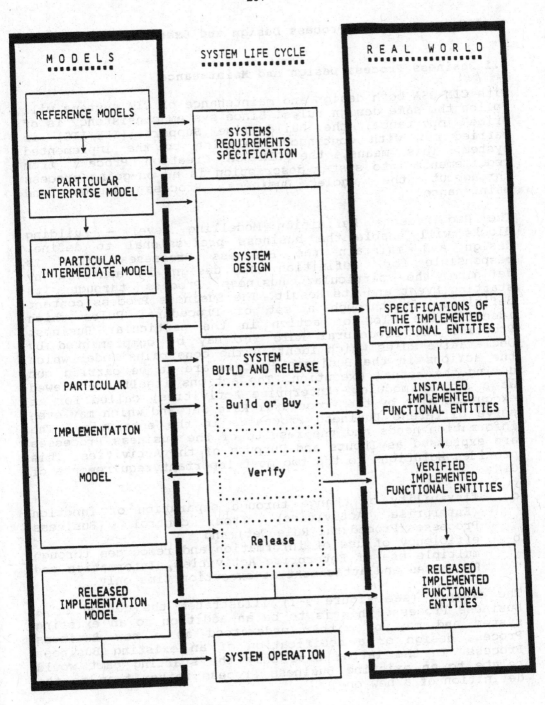

Figure 8-5: Relations of the CIM system Life Cycle

9. CIM-OSA Business Process Design and Execution

9.1 Business Process Design and Maintenance

With CIM-OSA both design and maintenance of CIM systems will
follow the same design rules. Since system consistency is of
prime importance, the Build Time Support (IEE/IIS) is
carried out with continuous relation to the implemented
system. This means, the CIM-OSA Creation Process from
requirements into system description is an on-going process
throughout the whole Business Process design and
maintenance.

The Requirements Definition Modelling Level - Building
Blocks will enable the business professional to define,
design and maintain the Business Processes s(he) is
responsible for. Definition and design is achieved by
defining the particular Business Process through its
starting Event and its Result. The Business Process content
definition is through a set of Procedural Rules which
identify the flow of action in the particular Business
Process. The Procedural Rule Set may be complemented by
Declarative Rules which identify the constrains under which
the actions in the Business Process are to be carried out
during the actual execution. The actions itself are viewed
as a set of modules (Enterprise Activities) called for at
execution time by the Procedural Rule Set and which may even
serve different Business Processes in the enterprise. The
information needs and the results of the Business Processes
are expressed as Inputs and Outputs of the Activities. This
provides solutions to the two most important requirements of
CIM:

o   flexibility of change through separation of function
     (Enterprise Activities) from control (Business
     Processes/Procedural Rule Set) and
o   efficiency of use of information and resources through
     multiple use of Enterprise Activities, Information and
     Resources and attachment at execution time only.

The example (see Figure 9-1) illustrates the design of a
Business Process. This is to be an addition to an existing
system and may be either understood as a new Business
Process design or a modification of an existing Business
Process. In the latter case only the starting part would
relate to an existing Business Process rather than to the
definition of a new one.

203

Business Professional	Build Time Support (IEE/IIS)
- start Business Process definition - select Bus. Proc. Type	- provide Business Process Design and Support Menu
- give Name - define Events and Result - define Responsibility	- register Type/Name/ID - register all Events and - register Result - register Responsibility
	- provide Procedural Rule Set Design and Supp. Menu - relate to Bus. Proc. ID
- design Proc. Rule Set	- check all defined Enterprise Activities - identify all not yet available Enterprise Activities
	- provide Enterprise Act. Design and Support Menu
- select Enterpr. Act. Type - give Enterp. Act. Name - define Responsibility	- register Type/ID/Name - register Responsibility
- identify Input/Output - define Responsibility	- check all defined I/O's - identify elements not yet available in Data Base t - register Responsibility - provide DB design support for missing DB elements
- design new DB elements (will require DB Professional) - define Responsibility	- register new DB elements - relate all DB elements to their I/O's - relate all I/O's to their Enterprise Activity - relate all Enterprise Activities to their Procedural Rule - register Responsibility
- quit Bus. Proc. design	

Figure 9-1: Design of a Business process

9.2 CIM-OSA Run Time - Business Process Execution

During the design process all CIM-OSA system components have been defined. For the execution of Business Processes the IT Run Time Support services (IEO/IIS) will be invoked. The execution of the business process will follow the Business Process control flow (Procedural Rule Set) defined during the design process.

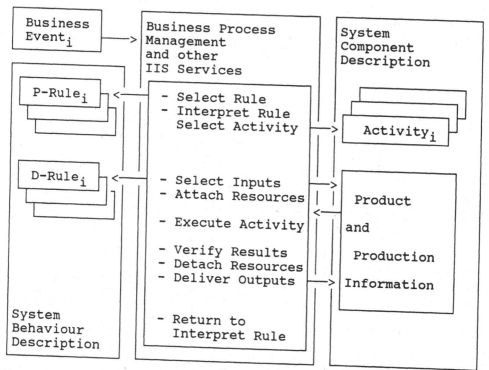

Figure 9-2: CIM-OSA Business Process execution

Figure 9-2 illustrates the execution of such a Business Process. The sequence of action carried out during this execution is summarized in the following:

1) **Business Process Events** (such as the receipt of a customer order) trigger the Business Process Management service of the CIM-OSA Integrated Data Processing Environment to execute a specific business process.

2) **Business Process Management** then
   A   selects the appropriate Procedural Rule Set,
   B   selects the appropriate Enterprise Activity,
   C   requests assignment of necessary resources,
   D   checks that the required information is available,
   E   passes control to the selected enterprise activity.

3)   The **Enterprise Activity** then
     A   carries out the desired function
     B   on completion or termination control is passed
           back the results of the activity to the
           information base
     C   it passes back control to Business Process
           Management along with the associated ending
           status.

4)   **Business Process Management** then
     A   selects the associated rule(s)
     B   according to the ending status selects the next
           enterprise activity for execution.

Note that the control linkage between Business Process
Management and the enterprise activity is implicit in the
Requirements Definition Model and as such is of no immediate
concern to the Business User creating the model (this
linkage is made explicit in the Implementation Description
Model).

9.3 Example of Business Process Design

A skeleton example of Business Process design is presented
below.   It addresses the area of Printed Circuit Board
design in the electronics industry.

The sequence of design activities is in accordance with the
description given in Figure 9-1. Only the activities to be
carried out by the business professional are described. IEE
actions are limited to hypothetical screen displays for menu
selection or user input. User actions (selections or inputs)
are emphasised on the screen displays.

To illustrate the Requirements Definition Model design, the
contents of the first 3 steps are presented.

9.3.1 Step 1: Select Business Process Type

Business Professional	Build Time Support (IEE/IIS)
start Business Process definition - select Bus. Proc. Type	- provide Business Process Design and Support Menu

```
┌─────────────────IEE Support Screen─────────────────┐
│ ┌─────────────────────────────────────────────────┐│
│ │ Select from BUSINESS PROCESS TYPES              ││
│ │ - Management/                                   ││
│ │ - Operation/Development/                        ││
│ │ - Support/                                      ││
└─┴─────────────────────────────────────────────────┴┘
```

9.3.2 Step 2: Identify Business Process Content

Business Professional	Build Time Support (IEE/IIS)
- give Name - define Events and Result - define Responsibility	- register Type/Name/ID - register all Events and - register Result - register Responsibility

Business process type will be taken over from the previous selection and the CIM-OSA ID will be provided by the ISE. All other inputs are user defined under ISE guidance (not shown). For simplicity; content of Event and Result not shown.

```
┌─────────────────IEE Design Screen─────────────────┐
│                                                    │
│  BUSINESS PROCESS                                  │
│  - Type:            Operational/Development        │
│  - CIM-OSA ID:      BP1.1.2                         │
│  - Name:            PCB Product Design             │
│  - TASK:            Define the mounted PCB          │
│  - Event:           Funct. Design Completed         │
│  - Result:          PCB Layout                      │
│  - Responsibility:  Head of PCB Design Dept.        │
│  - Proc. Rule:      PRS1.1.2                        │
│  - Decl. Rule:                                      │
│                                                    │
└────────────────────────────────────────────────────┘
```

9.3.3 Step 3: Design Procedural Rule Set

The Procedural Rule Set Type, Name and the CIM-OSA ID will be according to the selected Business Process Type and will be provided by the ISE.

Business Professional	Build Time Support (IEE/IIS)
	- provide Procedural Rule Set Design and Supp. Menu - relate to Bus. Proc. ID
- design Proc. Rule	- check all defined Enterprise Activities - identify all not yet available Enterprise Activities

```
┌─────────────────IEE Support Screen─────────────────┐
│                                                     │
│  Select from RELEVANT BUSINESS PROCESSES            │
│     none                                            │
│                                                     │
│  Select from RELEVANT ENTERPRISE ACTIVITY           │
│  - Operation/Development/Design                     │
│     EA014 Build and Match                           │
│     EA016 Wire (rout) Layers of PCB                 │
│  - Operation/Development/Verify                     │
│     EA017 Verify Wiring Rules                       │
│                                                     │
│  Select from PROCEDURAL RULE TYPES                  │
│  - SE Sequence       - FO Forced                    │
│  - SP Spawning       - GN Go/NoGO                   │
│  - RE Rendezvous     - CO Conditional               │
│                                                     │
└─────────────────────────────────────────────────────┘
```

```
┌─────────────────IEE Design Screen─────────────────┐
│                                                    │
│  PROCEDURAL RULE SET                               │
│  - Type:         Operational/Development           │
│  - Name:         PCB Product Design                │
│  - CIM-OSA ID: PRS1.1.2                            │
│  Content:                                          │
│  No Type Wait for Ending Status    Trigger         │
│  1  FO  Start      -               EA014           │
│  2  SE  EA014      - ok            EA015           │
│                    - Default       Term.&Report    │
│  3  SE  EA015      - ok            EA016           │
│                    - Default       Term.&Report    │
│  4  continued                                      │
│                                                    │
└────────────────────────────────────────────────────┘
```

9.4 Example of Business Process Execution

A part of the execution of the example Business Process given in the previous section is demonstrated below, using the execution framework presented in Figure 9-2.

9.4.1 Step 1: Start Business Process Execution

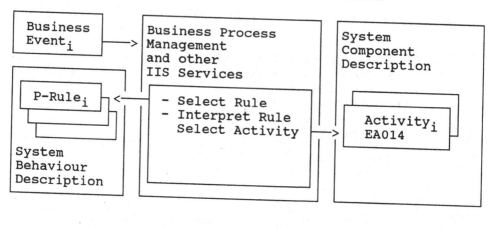

-Procedural Rule-

| 1 | Start | - | EA014 |

-Enterprise Activity-
```
Type : Operational, Develop, Design, Detail
Id.  : EA014
Name : Build & Match
```

9.4.2 Step 2: Select Enterprise Activity Inputs

All inputs are selected and all resources attached.

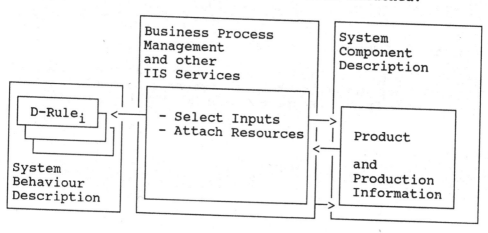

```
┌────────────Enterprise Activity────────────┐
│            CAD system - Layout subsystem   │
│ INPUTS                                     │
│ Primary  : FT,F view of PCB and sub-units  │
│ Secondary: BMY view of buildable functions │
│ Tertiary : Layout Specialist               │
│            CAD system - Layout subsystem   │
└────────────────────────────────────────────┘
```

10. Results from Standardisation Efforts

By its very nature and scope CIM-OSA provides a working basis for input to several standardisation areas, like:

o   Reference Architecture Models and Modelling Methods
o   Descriptive and Formal Languages
o   Industrial Automation
o   Integration of Heterogeneous Equipment

The results from the project work have been used on several occasions to introduce CIM-OSA into standardisation bodies on national and international level. These activities have mainly be carried out by project members who are also members of the relevant standard organisations.

Specific activities are listed in the following:

o   CIM-OSA has been introduced into ISO TC 184/SC5/WG1 on several occasions resulting in the inclusion of CIM-OSA in relevant reports (N61 and N95).

o   CIM-OSA has been introduced into the German DIN strategic CIM office (DIN Kommission CIM). As a result two working groups have taken CIM-OSA as a work item.

o   CIM-OSA has been introduced into the German NAM 96.5 Committee on Reference Models and Architecture. This group is waiting for further action from the AMICE project.

o   proposal to ISO TC184/SC5/WG1/N105

LIST OF FIGURES

1-1: The Expectations on Integration....................5
1-2: The Levels of Enterprise Integration..............6
1-3: CIM-OSA Modelling Approach.......................10
1-4: CIM-OSA Architectural Levels....................11
1-5: CIM-OSA Modelling Levels........................12
1-6: CIM-OSA Views..................................13
1-7: Overview of CIM-OSA Architectural Framework......14
1-8: Implementation of CIM-OSA......................15
1-9: CIM-OSA Information Technology Environments......16
1-10: CIM-OSA Particular Architecture.................19
1-11: Applying CIM-OSA - the CIM System Life Cycle.....21
2-1: Before AMICE...................................24
2-2: Starting AMICE.................................25
2-3: AMICE Project..................................26
2-4: After AMICE....................................27
3-1: Role of CIM-OSA................................34
4-1: Modelling Approach.............................37
4-2: Overview of Architectural Framework.............39
4-3: Levels of Genericity...........................40
4-4: Partial Level..................................41
4-5: Stepwise Instantiation.........................42
4-6: Levels of Modelling............................43
4-7: Stepwise Derivation Process....................44
4-8: Levels of Views................................45
4-9: Stepwise Generation Process....................46
5-1: CIM-OSA Modelling Levels and Derivation Process
      for CIM-OSA Particular Architecture.............52
5-2: Requirements Definition Model Building Blocks....54
5-3: Hierarchy of Business Processes.................56
5-4: Decomposition of Business Process...............58
5-5: Enterprise Activity............................60
5-6: Relationship between Stage Results..............61
5-7: Derivation of the Design Specification Model
      Function View..................................67
5-8: Relationship between Resource View and
      Organisation View..............................70
5-9: Content of the Implementation Description Model..71
5-10: Components described in the Implementation
      Description Model..............................72
5-11: Implementation Level Functional Decomposition
      of the CIM-OSA Enterprise......................76
5-12: Mapping the Design Specification Function View
      onto the Implementation Description Functional
      View...78
5-13: Cooperation of Functional Entities (partial
      refinement of Fig. 5-12).......................79
5-14: Derivation of the Implementation Description
      Model Information View.........................81

5-15: Implementation Description Model Resource View...83
5-16: Elements of the Implemented Organisation Model...84
5-17: Overview of CIM-OSA Environments.................86
6-1: Overview of CIM-OSA Constructs...................91
7-1: Behaviour of interacting Functional Entities....108
7-2: Graphical Symbols for Functional Diagrams.......110
7-3: Graphical Representation of Service Interfaces..111
7-4: Graphical Representation of Service System and
      Service Layer...................................111
7-5: Layering Model.................................113
7-6: Functional Model of a Client-Service
      Relationship....................................114
7-7: Linking the Client-Service Model with the
      Layering Model in the IIS.......................116
7-8: The Three Functional Areas of the IDPE.........117
7-9: IDPE Overview..................................119
7-10: Protocols and Layered Services used and
      provided by Communication Management............124
7-11: Protocols and Layered Services used and
      provided by System Wide Exchange................128
7-12: Protocols and Layered Services used and
      provided by System Wide Data....................131
7-13: Protocols and Layered Services used and
      provided by Data Management.....................134
7-14: Protocols and Layered Services used and
      provided by the Machine Front End...............140
7-15: Human Front End as part of the CIM-OSA
      Integrating Infrastructure......................145
7-16: Internal Structure of Human Front End..........147
7-17: Protocols and Layered Services used and
      provided by the Human Front End.................152
7-18: Protocols and Layered Services used and
      provided by the Application Front End...........160
7-19: Protocols and Layered Services used and
      provided by the Business Process Control........167
7-20: Protocols and Layered Services used and
      Provided by the Activity Control................172
7-21: Protocols and Layered Services used and
      provided by the Resource Management.............179
7-22: Standardisation of Reference Architectures......182
8-1: Overlapping Product Life Cycles................183
8-2: The Life Cycle of a Business Process...........185
8-3: Relationships between the two Life Cycles......186
8-4: System Life Cycle..............................187
8-5: Relations of the CIM system Life Cycle.........194
9-1: Design of a Business process...................196
9-2: CIM-OSA Business Process execution.............197

Printed in the United States
By Bookmasters